GEORGE WASHINGTON

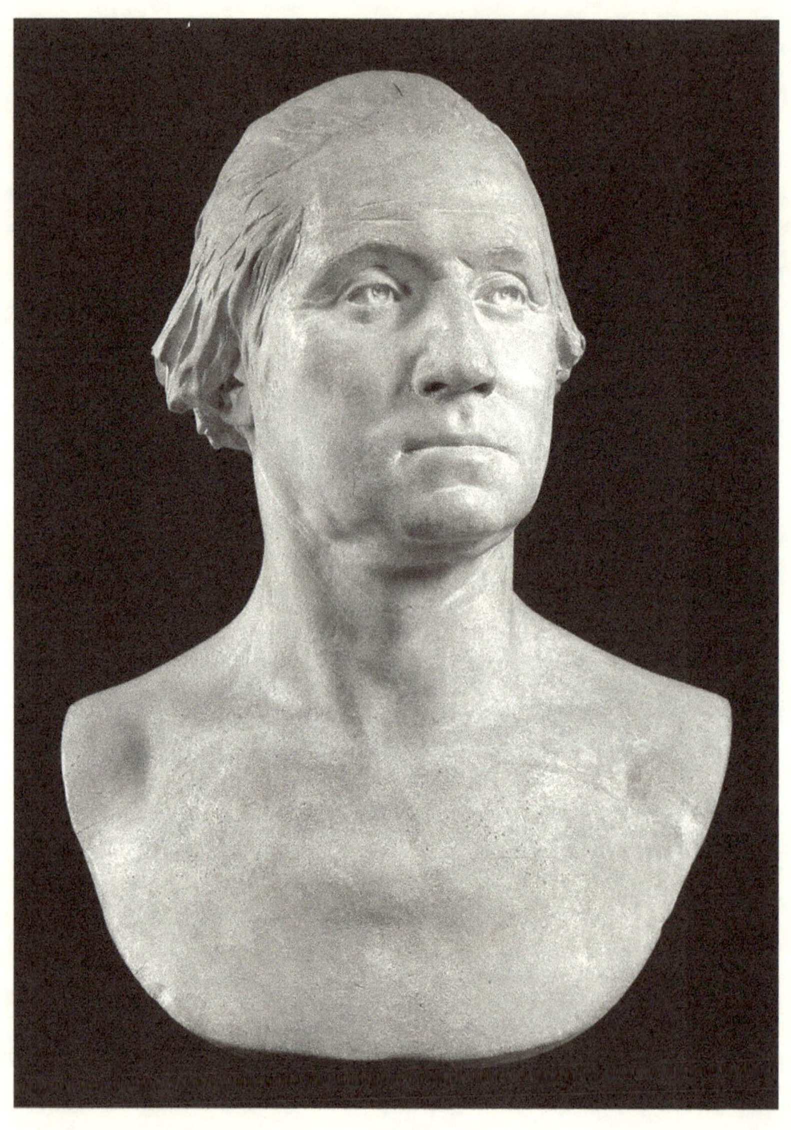

GEORGE WASHINGTON

His Quest for Honor and Fame

Peter R. Henriques

UNIVERSITY OF VIRGINIA PRESS
Charlottesville and London

The University of Virginia Press is situated on the traditional lands of the Monacan Nation, and the Commonwealth of Virginia was and is home to many other Indigenous people. We pay our respect to all of them, past and present. We also honor the enslaved African and African American people who built the University of Virginia, and we recognize their descendants. We commit to fostering voices from these communities through our publications and to deepening our collective understanding of their histories and contributions.

University of Virginia Press

Printed in the United States of America on acid-free paper

First published 2025

1 3 5 7 9 8 6 4 2

LIBRARY OF CONGRESS CATALOGING-IN-PUBLICATION DATA
Names: Henriques, Peter R., author
Title: George Washington : his quest for honor and fame / Peter R. Henriques.
Description: Charlottesville : University of Virginia Press, 2025. |
Includes bibliographical references and index.
Identifiers: LCCN 2025008597 (print) | LCCN 2025008598 (ebook) |
ISBN 9780813954189 hardback | ISBN 9780813954196 ebook
Subjects: LCSH: Washington, George, 1732–1799 | Washington, George, 1732–1799—Psychology | Washington, George, 1732–1799—Ethics | Slavery—United States—History—18th century | Presidents—United States—Biography | BISAC: BIOGRAPHY & AUTOBIOGRAPHY / Presidents & Heads of State | HISTORY / United States / Revolutionary Period (1775–1800) | LCGFT: Biographies
Classification: LCC E312.25 .H46 2025 (print) | LCC E312.25 (ebook) |
DDC 973.4/1092 $a B—dc23/eng/20250407
LC record available at https://lccn.loc.gov/2025008597
LC ebook record available at https://lccn.loc.gov/2025008598

Frontispiece: Bust of George Washington, Jean-Antoine Houdon, 1785. (Mount Vernon Ladies' Association)

Cover art: Washington at the Battle of Princeton, published by Chappell, Johnson, Fry & Co., 1857. (Courtesy of the Mount Vernon Ladies' Association)
Cover design: Cecilia Sorochin

For Marlene, my wife of over sixty years.
Through good times and not so good times,
you have always been the love of my life.

From an early age George Washington felt a compelling desire to be seen, admired, honored, and, above all else, to be remembered.

Indeed, my dear General, it must be a pleasing reflection to you . . . to find that history, poetry, painting, & sculpture will vie with each other in consigning your name to immortality.

—DAVID HUMPHREYS,
Washington's wartime aide and biographer

CONTENTS

AUTHOR'S NOTE

If anyone had told me in summer of 2023 that I would be writing one more book on George Washington, I would have expressed extreme skepticism. I had my final project concerning Washington firmly in my mind. In collaboration with Ron Hurst, my good friend and senior vice president of education and historic resources at Colonial Williamsburg, I had, over the course of a dozen years, the privilege of presenting approximately thirty different talks in that wonderful historical setting. We concluded that my final undertaking in that regard would be to present a series of seven lectures in the fall of 2023 examining what I view as seven distinct stages of George Washington's life. Frankly, the talks succeeded well beyond my own expectations—enough so that, backed by the gentle urging of my wife, Marlene, I began to seriously consider the idea of reshaping those presentations into the core of a very brief interpretative biography. With the encouragement and support of Nadine Zimmerli, editor in chief of the University of Virginia Press, this book is the result.

Understanding this volume's origin matters for at least two reasons. The first is that my goal in writing and delivering those presentations was not to present some new information or unveil completely original insights about George Washington, although I do believe that my intense focus on his desire for honor and fame differentiates my work from those who see that desire as simply one of many factors. Rather, my goal was to summarize my many years spent studying George Washington and incorporate the best of Washington scholarship into a brief, readable, scholarly book for people who wish to better understand America's most important statesman.

A second reason to understand the origin of this book is that I gave those seven talks at Colonial Williamsburg without any expectation that they would ever be published. I have always been an eclectic borrower. If I find that someone has said what I wanted to say and said it better than I might have, I am comfortable in using those words. Naturally, I always want to credit such sources and have tried to do so in this book. Nevertheless, I don't doubt that I have failed to do so in some cases. I apologize in advance if anyone finds that I failed to give proper acknowledgment for a quote or concept. Please recognize that is due to the less than perfect memory of an octogenarian rather than to any intent to claim someone else's words or ideas as my own.

Also, at the forceful urging of both excellent reviewers of the draft of the book, and because the topic is so timely, I have added an afterword on George Washington and slavery. I don't want to imply that "afterword" means the topic is not central to a biography of George Washington. It is, but I found it impossible to give it proper attention by weaving it into a very brief biography.

Finally, to those who say, "not another work on George Washington," my response is that because of both his importance and his complexity, George Washington will merit new biographers far into the future.

INTRODUCTION

GEORGE WASHINGTON DIED SUDDENLY on December 14, 1799.[1] Conveyed only by word of mouth and the limited print media of the day, news of his death nonetheless spread with remarkable speed. It was almost as if everyone's father had died at the same time. A Boston newspaper described the news as "agonizing." Black mourning ribbon became impossible to find. Between December 1799 and February 1800, no fewer than 440 eulogies were delivered to portions of a population that could not get enough of Washington. The most famous was by Henry Lee. Speaking in Philadelphia, Lee declared Washington to have been "First in War, First in Peace, and First in the Hearts of his Countrymen." The Reverend Richard Allen, founder of the African Methodist Church, told his congregation its members "had particular cause to bemoan our loss" because Washington had been a "sympathizing friend and tender father."[2] From Natchez to New Haven, speakers declared Washington "the American Moses," proudly above such lesser men as Julius Caesar, Alexander the Great, Oliver Cromwell, and Napoleon.[3] The nation's creation had relied on a pantheon of six men in particular, and each of the surviving four—Hamilton, Adams,

Jefferson, and Madison—and Franklin before his death in 1790 hailed the fallen Washington as their better, the only indispensable figure in the country's founding.

His passing rocked Europe as well. Napoleon ordered French battle standards draped in black and Washington's bust placed in the Tuileries Palace alongside that nation's modern and ancient heroes. Even in Great Britain, whose army Washington had bested in battle, expressions of praise and respect were numerous.

Who was this man who achieved such a remarkable historical impact? How did a son of a second marriage in a second-tier family of the Virginia gentry, denied a formal education and lacking a large inheritance, gain such renown and become the most consequential figure in the founding of the United States?

Attempting to answer these two questions will guide this brief interpretive biography. This is not a Wikipedia-style biography, nor is it a eulogistic biography. Indeed, it saddens me to see that the most successful statesman in American history is often best remembered as a boy with a hatchet or a simple-minded prig kneeling in the snow to pray.[4] It is certainly not an indictment of Washington for failing to be as progressive as many modern commentators think he should have been. It is obviously not a complete biography.

I hope readers will reach a better understanding of George Washington by reading this book, but I by no means claim to "know" the real George Washington. He was a remarkably complex individual, and although he wanted to be famous, he did not want to be truly known. To that end, he was very guarded in much of his correspondence, the more so as his fame grew. Washington is determined to tell us what he did but equally determined not to tell us what he thought about it.

From an early age, George Washington felt a compelling desire to be seen, admired, honored, and, above all else, to be remembered. While this characterization would certainly apply to many of the founders,[5] it particularly applies to George Washington. None of the other founders wrote that he would "envy" a death at any age as long as that death gave birth to honor and glorious memory. None of his illustrious compatriots went to great expense and effort to present themselves in a manner to perfectly fit whatever situation he encountered. None was as sensitive to criticism and slights, actual or perceived, to his honor. Just as the Rosetta Stone enabled scholars to grasp and decode the meaning of ancient Egyptian writing, this insight will help readers to better understand George Washington and the forces that drove him throughout his remarkable life.

1
YOUNG MAN ON THE MAKE

1732–1754

THE TASK OF EXAMINING George Washington's early years is complex. We possess an inordinate amount of information about Washington from the beginning of the French and Indian War in 1754 until his death in December 1799, but of his earlier years we know precious little. The University of Virginia is compiling the definitive edition of *The Papers of George Washington.* Approximately seventy-seven volumes, averaging six hundred–plus pages each, have been published, with about thirteen volumes to come. Material on Washington's life before 1754 comprises the first sixty-two pages of the first volume. In short, there is a tremendous amount about Washington's youth that we do not know and that we will never know, making those early years fertile ground for myths and legends.

George Washington's birth is carefully recorded in the family Bible: "George Washington Son to Augustine & Mary his wife was born the 11th day of February 1731/2 about 10 in the morning & was Baptized the 5th of April following." What makes this entry extraordinary is that Washington himself wrote it on some undetermined date.[1] This fact emphasizes that Washington was a recordkeeping animal, and one with "an uncommon awareness of himself." The volume and range of Washington's prerevolutionary war papers mark his archives as those of someone who derived great satisfaction from organizing, setting down, and preserving a detailed record of his own existence.

Perhaps the most revealing example is a remarkably lengthy and detailed document which somehow has survived the passage of time. In it, the teenaged Washington describes a coat he had seen and which he wanted replicated for himself. His painstaking comments total over 150 words!

> Memorandum to have my Coat made by the following Directions to be made a Frock with a Lapel Breast the Lapel to Contain on each side six Button Holes and to be about 5 or 6 Inches wide all the way equal and to turn as the Breast on the Coat does to have it made very Long Waisted and in Length to come down to or below the Bent of the knee the Waist from the armpit to the Fold to be exactly as long or Longer than from thence to the Bottom not to have more than one fold in the Skirt and the top to be made just to turn in and three Button Holes the Lapel at the top to turn as the Cape of the Coat and Bottom to Come Parallel with the Button Holes the Last Button hole in the Breast to be right opposite to the Button on the Hip.[2]

Washington's intense concern with appearances and acute interest in his image as seen by others is present from very early in his life.

Six key events marked Washington's first twenty-two years. They are his father's death, his relationship with his mother, his connection to the Fairfax family, his trip to Barbados, his appointment as Governor Dinwiddie's envoy to warn the French to stay out of the Ohio Valley, and his commission as lieutenant colonel of the First Virginia Regiment.

No serious author is going to write at any length about George's relationship with his father, Augustine, who was often away and who died when George was only eleven. It is surprising, in the reams upon reams of Washington's papers, how infrequently he makes even fleeting

George Washington as a young surveyor. (Mount Vernon Ladies' Association)

mention of his father, and never in a reflective manner. There is not even enough material for informed historical speculation.

That said, Augustine Washington's death clearly and profoundly influenced his son's life. George was the firstborn son and eldest of five surviving children from his father's second marriage. The boy's older half brothers, Lawrence and Augustine, received the major portions of their father's estate, subjecting his widow, Mary Ball Washington, and her five children to financial stress and dashing any expectation that George would be following his half brothers to Appleby School in

England. In time, George was to inherit ten enslaved workers, a few hundred worn-out acres of land, and the family home at Ferry Farm, which had been damaged by fire a few years earlier. Basically, he would have to make his own way in the world.

Most significantly, George became the man of the house at the tender age of eleven. That experience was difficult and left permanent scars. He had to learn to deal with his mother, Mary Ball Washington, a powerful, strong-willed, independent, and demanding yet deeply insecure woman who came to see her oldest son's true duty to be attending to her many needs.[3] She resented anything that distracted him from her. Underneath her seeming independence, Mary was a needy woman wracked by abandonment issues. In widowhood, she probably turned to her eldest child as an emotional crutch or as an unusual sort of best friend.

His upbringing left George Washington with insecurities of his own. He never was able to obtain his mother's unalloyed approval, nor could he satisfy this parent, so lavish in her demands and so stingy with her praise. One of George Washington's most salient traits was an extreme sensitivity to criticism and an intense desire for approval, which was perhaps a corollary of his aching need to win the admiration of others. He feared criticism in a way that he never feared enemy bullets. It is reasonable to posit that what became an endless quest for approval arose at least in part from his relationship with his demanding and never completely satisfied mother.

In recent years, Mary's reputation has suffered at the hands of many Washington scholars—most recently Ron Chernow—but the picture is more complex than Chernow indicates.[4] Washington's later correspondence makes clear that though his mother certainly could be difficult, she also played a central and occasionally positive role in his rise.

Having no father to serve as a patron and with only limited financial resources in Virginia's deeply hierarchical and patriarchal society, young George, in order to advance, had no alternative except to ally himself with men of years and wealth—and he did forge such alliances.

The great Virginia historian Douglas Southall Freeman explained why: "Powerful Virginia elders, who saw much loose living and indolence around them, found stimulation and reassurance in a young man of unassailed morals and of mature, sound judgment, who was full of energetic vigor."[5] Young Washington could hardly have attracted such enthusiastic notice if he were clumsy or socially inept or a libertine. Certainly, considerable credit for George's early success must go to his mother, and Mary deserves admiration and praise for what she accomplished. As her great-grandson George Washington Parke Custis observed, she taught her son "the duties of obedience . . . the levity and indulgence, common to youth, were tempered by a deference and . . . restraint."[6]

And she kept the adolescent George from joining the Royal Navy, a path endorsed by both Lawrence Washington and Colonel William Fairfax. How different American history might have been had Mary not had the temerity and strength of character to resist the directives of such worldly males. And her apron strings, while strong, were not chronically entangling. Soon after squelching the navy scheme, she agreed to let George undertake his first great adventure, an expedition across the Blue Ridge Mountains and into the Shenandoah Valley as a member of the Fairfax surveying party.

Undoubtedly, she believed such a sojourn would advance his prospects. And George Washington was desperately eager to advance his prospects. Washington's yearning for public honor gnawed at him all his life. From an early age, he hungered to rank among the great Virginia planters. In Paul Longmore's perceptive words, "Throughout his life, the ambition for distinction spun inside George Washington like a dynamo, generating the astounding energy with which he produced his greatest historical achievement—himself."[7]

He was lucky to have excellent role models close at hand. Most scholars declare that the most important was his older half brother Lawrence. Fourteen years George's senior, Lawrence is depicted as a surrogate father, a man young George idolized and on whom he modeled himself. No doubt Lawrence was very important, and his military career under Admiral Edward Vernon in the unsuccessful attack on Cartagena most likely stirred dreams of military action and glory in George, but I believe Lawrence's admirers exaggerate his influence. It is worth noting that Lawrence attempted to remove the Reverend Charles Green from Truro Parish for allegedly sexually assaulting Lawrence's young wife, Anne Fairfax, in the years before their marriage. The ecclesiastical trial cleared Reverend Green,[8] and Lawrence was defeated in his bid to be vestryman in Truro Parish. Significantly, George Washington, despite Lawrence's deep antipathy to Green, later befriended the accused clergyman and tried to help his widow when she fell upon hard times. Would he have done so if he had uncritically accepted Lawrence's charges against Green? Washington's divergent conclusion on such a major point suggests that his admiration for Lawrence was not as fulsome as generally portrayed.

Seen through the historian's lone advantage, hindsight, Lawrence's greatest gift to and impact on his half brother was to introduce George to two great patrons, Colonel William Fairfax and Governor Robert Dinwiddie. These men of position and substance opened doors that otherwise would have been closed to George, despite his drive and determination.

A few months after inheriting Mount Vernon upon his father's death, Lawrence married William Fairfax's daughter, Anne. Only fifteen years old, the bride was perhaps the most eligible young woman in northern Virginia. Colonel William Fairfax, cousin to Thomas, Sixth Lord Fairfax, was Thomas's land agent for the entire Northern Neck, a holding that then exceeded five million acres. William Fairfax was the master of Belvoir, a beautiful plantation approximately four miles south of Mount Vernon. He was a power in the upper house of the Virginia House of Burgesses, a twelve-man roster known as the King's Council, and the most important man in northern Virginia.

Through visits to Lawrence, George was often at Belvoir, where he learned much of what it meant to be a true Virginia gentleman. As a young student, George had not only written out the "Rules of Civility" but worked hard to live by these precepts defining proper behavior in a hierarchical society. These maxims originated in the late sixteenth century in France and were popularly circulated during Washington's time. They included guidelines for behavior in pleasant company, appropriate actions in formal situations, and general courtesies. The Fairfax family, including the alluring Sally Cary Fairfax, in effect served as young Washington's finishing school.

One of young Washington's talents was the assiduous courting of powerful men. Colonel William Fairfax did more than anyone else to open doors for young Washington, whom he treated as a protégé, if not as a surrogate son. Later Washington would declare he was under "many obligations" to the colonel,[9] "for whose memory and friendship I shall ever retain a most grateful sense."[10] He made a special effort, despite being involved in a war, to attend his funeral in 1757.

It was most likely William Fairfax who invited Washington to join that surveying trip in 1748, and almost all of the 190 surveys done by young Washington between the ages of seventeen and twenty were on Fairfax land. The Western journey exposed Washington to a fresh country of almost unimaginable richness. The vision he formed of a spacious Western frontier would influence him as a land speculator and eventually as an advocate of American nationhood. And it was almost certainly due to the influence of William, and of Thomas, Sixth Lord Fairfax, who was also partial to him, that Washington was appointed official surveyor for Culpeper County. His appointment was exceptional both because of his youth—he was only seventeen—and because he skipped the standard path of service as an apprentice or deputy to a county surveyor. He earned his first job the old-fashioned way—through powerful friends.

Washington's venture into surveying seems a very logical pursuit for a young man having to make his own living. Early on, as his schoolbook exercises demonstrate, Washington showed proficiency in mathematics and drawing, and even his earliest surveys are surprisingly precise and detailed. Today, a surveyor is a skilled tradesman who typically works at roadside, but eighteenth-century colonial society viewed surveyors as professionals, comparable to lawyers, physicians, and clergymen, and recognized them as gentry. Surveyors formed a corps of second-tier leaders, influential at the county level and numbering among the colony's practical-minded intellectual elite.

Washington's four-year career as a professional surveyor both revealed and inclined him to adopt lifelong traits: precision, systematic analysis, self-discipline, perseverance, industriousness, acceptance of responsibility, and especially alertness to commercial advantage. Surveying alerted him to the extraordinary business opportunities abundant in those virgin lands. He used his surveyor's fees to buy choice tracts, laying the foundation for what would eventually become a very extensive landed estate of over fifty thousand acres. Swift appraisal of the tangible would always be his mental forte. By the time he was twenty-one, he was earning £100 or more a year for part-time work as a surveyor and owned over two thousand acres of land in the lower Shenandoah Valley. No theme appears more frequently in Washington's writings than his love for land, especially his own land.

George's surveying was interrupted by the failing health of Lawrence, who had contracted tuberculosis during the Cartagena campaign under Admiral Edward Vernon several years earlier. Seeking a healthier climate, in 1751 Lawrence, with George as a traveling companion and perhaps caregiver, journeyed to the island of Barbados in the West Indies, the younger Washington's only trip outside of what would become the United States.

That three-month sojourn changed his life.[11] On it he contracted and survived smallpox, acquiring lifelong immunity against the dreaded disease. More subtly, he dined in the glittering company of commodores, admirals, judges, wealthy merchants, and Tortola's governor. He spent evenings in conversations with high-ranking British officers. He observed some of the most extensive fortifications in British America, no doubt further stimulating his interest in a military career.

Sickening further, Lawrence veered off alone for medical help in Bermuda. George returned to Virginia bearing a letter from Lawrence addressed to the new governor of Virginia, Robert Dinwiddie. That introduction began a connection crucial to the younger Washington's career. His ability to enlist powerful older men's enthusiastic support cannot be overestimated.

Dinwiddie had reason to be impressed by young Washington, whom the governor described as a "young person of distinction."[12] Part of the package was Washington's physical presence, characterized a few years later:

> He may be described as being straight as an Indian, measuring 6 feet 2 inches in his stockings, and weighing 175 lbs. . . . His frame is padded with well-developed muscles, indicating great strength. . . . His head is well shaped, though not large, but is gracefully poised on a superb neck. A large and straight rather than a prominent nose; bluegrey penetrating eyes which are widely separated and overhung by a heavy brow. His face is long rather than broad, with high round cheek bones, and terminates in a good firm chin. . . . A pleasing and benevolent tho a commanding countenance, dark brown hair which he wears in a cue. . . . His features are regular and placid with all the muscles of his face under perfect control, tho flexible and expressive of deep feeling when moved by emotions. In conversation he looks you full in the face, is deliberate, deferential and engaging. His demeanor at all times composed and dignified. His movements and gestures are graceful, his walk majestic, and he is a splendid horseman.[13]

Washington's equestrian skill in a horse-worshipping society was a major plus, as was his skill as a dancer. His physical grace, enhanced by taking fencing lessons, was an important part of the personal presence and charisma that from early on so riveted those who met him.

Governor Dinwiddie had another motive for favoring young Washington: He needed the political backing of Colonel William Fairfax, now presiding over the Virginia Council and seeming almost as committed to son-in-law Lawrence's younger sibling as to Lawrence. Until illness forced his retirement, Lawrence had held the very lucrative position of adjutant general for the Virginia militia. The decision was made to divide the colony into four militia districts, each with its own adjutant. Despite his youth—he was only twenty—and complete lack of military experience beyond fencing lessons and informal reading, George sought the adjutancy for northern Virginia. He had to settle for the southern district and its £100 annual salary until, at his urging, friends in the House of Burgesses helped engineer his appointment to the northern district. The young Washington could be alternatively fawning and assertive, appealingly modest and distressingly pushy. He was now Major Washington.

A much more important appointment soon loomed. Both Great Britain and France, the two superpowers of the eighteenth century, claimed the Ohio Country—the region comprising present-day Ohio and Indiana, along with parts of western Pennsylvania and West Virginia. Both nations had vague ambitions for that vast tract, of course basically ignoring Native American claims to the region. Until about the middle of the century neither great power was in a position to assert control over the area. The French sent major exploring parties into this region, while in Virginia a group of expansionists—its ranks included Lawrence Washington, William Fairfax, and Governor Dinwiddie—formed the Ohio Company. The partners stood to profit handsomely as the Crown promised the Company half a million acres of land if the enterprise was able to build a fort and within a given time settle the region.

Knowing France also claimed the territory, Dinwiddie, now acting governor, sought permission and advice from London on how best to proceed. Whitehall replied in mid-October 1753 with the answer Dinwiddie desired: "You are to require of Them peaceably to depart."

Washington Crossing the Allegany River, painted by D. Huntington, engraved by D. Kimberly, 1844. (Mount Vernon Ladies' Association)

They added that if France stood fast, "We do hereby strictly charge, and command You, to drive them off by Force of arms."[14] Dinwiddie needed an envoy to carry that message to the French and in the process better ascertain their intentions for the region.

With historical hindsight, it is clear that Dinwiddie's choice of George Washington as that emissary was one of the most profoundly decisive moments of Washington's entire life. At first glance, he seems an unlikely candidate for so crucial a mission. He was only twenty-one, spoke no French, and lacked even a scintilla of diplomatic training. Yet Washington had the firm support of his major patron, William Fairfax of Belvoir, and that of the governor, as well as a strong physique and, courtesy of surveying, the necessary field experience. Colonel Fairfax almost certainly alerted him to the opportunity. Washington jumped at the chance to enhance his reputation and "offered himself to go" as the governor's envoy. His commission from Dinwiddie to the French read in part, "I reposing especial trust and confidence in the Ability, Conduct & Fidelity of you the said George Washington."[15]

Washington's mission to deliver Dinwiddie's letter to the commandant of French forces in the Ohio Country was the stuff of future legend. The expedition was to be a nearly nine-hundred-mile winter journey through a region that most Virginians regarded as a howling wilderness. Braving terrible weather, almost unbearable cold, forbidding forests, uncertain Indian allies, and French resistance if not outright treachery, Washington survived an apparent assassination attempt by an Indian guide. He nearly drowned when his raft capsized on the frigid Allegheny River. From that perilous night forward, one senses Washington beginning to see himself as a major character in life's drama, always alert to how his experiences would play in the sitting rooms of Belvoir Manor, in the chambers of the gubernatorial palace, and ultimately on the stage of history.[16]

After what he called "as fatiguing a journey as it is possible to conceive," he reported to Governor Dinwiddie in January 1754 that the French totally rejected Great Britain's claims and were making plans to seize and hold the critical but yet totally undeveloped land at the Forks of the Ohio River (present-day Pittsburgh). In the words of Washington's journal, "They told me it was their absolute Design to take Possession of the Ohio, & by G— they would do it."[17] His journal, at Dinwiddie's request, was quickly published to considerable acclaim in both America and Great Britain. The House of Burgesses awarded him a sizable bonus of £50 as an expression of appreciation for his difficult undertaking. The young George Washington was becoming noteworthy.

Major Washington soon lobbied for and was promoted to be second in command of the newly formed Virginia Regiment. His approach in a letter to Richard Corbin, an influential member of the Council, is revealing. In that epistolary quest for a high military position at so young an age, his ambition shines through the cloak of modesty in which he couches his case—"humble bragging," we might say today. The letter bespeaks the drive for distinction and the enduring fear of failure that would remain central themes all his life. To command the regiment "is a charge too great for my youth and inexperience to be entrusted with. Knowing this, I have too sincere a love for my country, to undertake that which may tend to the prejudice of it. But if I could entertain hopes that you thought me worthy of the post of Lieutenant-colonel, and would favor me so far as to mention it at the appointment of officers, I could not but entertain a true sense of the kindness."[18] The disclaimer itself emitted a whiff of audacity, but he soon received his commission.

One biography of young Washington describes him as "an ordinary young man" in extraordinary times.[19] The evidence clearly points to the contrary. George Washington's accomplishments by the time he was twenty-two are truly impressive:

—Official surveyor for Culpeper County by age seventeen.
—Owner of over two thousand acres of land.
—Earning in excess of £100 per year from part-time work surveying.
—Adjutant of the militia for the southern—and soon the northern—district of Virginia at age twenty with a salary of another £100 a year.
—A special envoy to the French at age twenty-one. His efforts were rewarded with a bonus from the House of Burgesses and publication of his journal in both Virginia and Great Britain.
—Won the patronage of Colonel William Fairfax, Governor Robert Dinwiddie, Richard Corbin, and William Fitzhugh, among other powerful men.
Inducted into a new Masonic Lodge in Fredericksburg at age twenty and elevated to "Master Mason" at age twenty-one.

In the spring of 1754, the Virginia House of Burgesses voted funds to raise a regiment of three hundred men to protect settlers in the

Ohio Country from the mounting French threat. Workers for the Ohio Company had already begun to build a fort at the strategic location where the Allegheny and Monongahela Rivers merge into the Ohio River. Now commissioned a lieutenant colonel for the newly formed Virginia Regiment, Washington was ordered to raise and lead men to protect the fortification project.

While confident that the British must and would control this key real estate, he quickly found enthusiasm for the enterprise scant and pickings for the troops slim. Washington complained vociferously about the quality of the available recruits. "We daily Experience the great necessity for Cloathing the Men, as we find the generallity of those who are to be Enlisted, are of those loose, Idle Persons that are quite destitute of House, and Home, and I may say many of them of Cloaths," he wrote to Governor Dinwiddie. "There is many of them without Shoes, other's want Stockings, some are without Shirts, and not a few that have Scarce a Coat, or Waistcoat, to their Backs; in short they are as illy provided as can well be conceiv'd."[20] An elitist by nature and circumstance, he bemoaned what a difficult task it was to "manage a number of selfwill'd, ungovernable People," a theme he would reprise on numerous occasions.

Despite the challenges, in April 1754 Washington marched his motley band of 160 soldiers to Winchester on the way to the Forks of the Ohio to protect the workers and the new bastion they were constructing. Doubtless, Washington thought if carrying the British ultimatum to the French a year earlier had won him favor, taking to the field at the head of an independent military command stood to be more dazzling still.

A key moment in George Washington's life was fast approaching with far-reaching ramifications not only for him but for the wider world.

2

A FRUSTRATING WAR AND A SUCCESSFUL MARRIAGE

1754–1759

THESE YEARS FIND George Washington encountering more negative commentary from historians than in the rest of his life combined. That is because he is on the center stage—where he wants very much to be—but without the skills or self-control needed to succeed at that level.[1] He desired to be both a warrior and a gentleman but had yet to reconcile the contradictory demands of self-assertion and courtesy. While he demonstrated hints of potential for greatness, he was unable to rein in his "tumultuous passions." Remarkably brave, charismatic, and highly capable, he was also temperamental, vain, thin-skinned, petulant, demanding, stubborn, annoying, hasty, and passionate.[2] His five years of service during the French and Indian War were characterized, on the one hand, by reckless risk-taking, insubordination, and whining and, on the other, by the methodical molding of an unruly, inexperienced provincial force into a semiprofessional regiment whose performance impressed British Regulars.

Despite the difficulties, in the spring of 1754 Lieutenant Colonel Washington marched his unimpressive band of about 160 soldiers to Winchester and onward toward the bastion under construction at the Forks of the Ohio River. To Washington's great frustration, when he arrived at Winchester, the promised wagons and teamsters were nowhere to be found. Considering the nature of the emergency, the young colonel took matters into his own hands. The lengths to which he was willing to go are indicated by a warrant for his arrest, issued by the Frederick County clerk on April 15, 1754, on charges of trespassing.[3] After failing to serve the warrant, the sheriff noted on its reverse side that "the within named George Washington would not be taken. He kept me off by force of arms"!

Washington soon learned of a significant new development. The French forces had advanced from their northern strongholds in sufficient strength to take control of the vital Forks of the Ohio River, although they allowed the beleaguered workmen to return unharmed to Virginia. Eschewing the caution the changed circumstances warranted, the callow young officer proceeded toward the fort, seemingly eager to engage the French. It is unclear what Washington hoped to accomplish by continuing to press his men forward toward the Ohio River. Perhaps a contemporary critic had it right: His action resulted from his "being too ambitious of acquiring all the honor, or as much as he could, before the rest joined him."[4] His rash decision had unforeseen consequences.

While at Great Meadows, about forty miles south of the Forks of the Ohio, scouts sent by his Indian ally, Tanaghrisson, or Half King, as he was known to the British, reported a body of French troops not far from his camp. Jumping to the conclusion that the Frenchmen intended to attack him, Washington decided to strike first. His baptism by fire, the brief clash at Jumonville Glen, named for the leader of this small French party, occurred on May 28, 1754. Not surprisingly, accounts of the brief skirmish vary dramatically, although in a fairly recently discovered account, one of Washington's Native American allies explicitly asserts that it was George Washington himself who fired the first shot.[5] Caught completely unaware, the French were quickly subdued, whereupon Jumonville himself was brutally slain by Half King.

The Jumonville Affair and Washington's later capitulation at Fort Necessity shed the first blood of what would become known as the

The Virginia Colonel, Charles Volkmar, after Charles Willson Peale, 1874. (Mount Vernon Ladies' Association)

Seven Years' War, commonly referred to in America as the French and Indian War. As the great British statesman Sir Horace Walpole wrote, "The volley fired by a young Virginian in the backwoods of America set the world on fire."[6] In one of history's greatest ironies, the man who literally fired the shot that triggered truly epic events—France's eviction from North America, the American War of Independence, and the French Revolution—in the final analysis ended up being the most famous and revered figure of the entire age. In the short term, the ensuing events revealed just how much George Washington had to learn about conducting military operations.

The French claimed that Jumonville had been on a diplomatic mission comparable to Washington's foray the previous year. Now

Jumonville had been wantonly murdered, and the French vowed revenge. Whatever private misgivings or doubts Washington may have had, his public pronouncements were defensive and arrogant, and privately, he seemed to have found the thrill of battle exciting. He confided to his brother Jack, "I heard Bullets whistle and believe me there was something charming in the sound."[7] Not many men are wired that way. He boasted to Governor Dinwiddie, "If the whole Detachment of the French behave with no more Resolution than this chosen Party did, I flatter myself we shall have no great trouble in driving them to ... [damn] Montreal."[8] He certainly did flatter himself. These were the boastful words of a young and inexperienced leader with little sense of the realities he was facing.

The French quickly mounted a counterattack by a force of French troops and Indians totaling about seven hundred men led by Jumonville's irate brother. Washington's augmented but still small force of several hundred men soon found themselves holed up in a quickly constructed fort, aptly named Fort Necessity. Losing more than a third of his men the first day, Colonel Washington had every reason to expect his own life might end the next day—July 4—when the French stormed his inadequate bastion.

Rather than storming the fort, however, the French were willing to parley. Fearing that enemy reinforcements were close by, the French commander decided to seek Washington's sword rather than his life. He offered to allow Washington and his men to capitulate and return to Virginia if Washington signed a document agreeing that the French had mounted the attack only to avenge the assassination of their minister. The document was in French, the night was rainy, and Washington's translator was less than perfectly fluent in French. Nevertheless, in signing the document, Washington unwittingly gave the French a great diplomatic and propaganda victory, for he essentially admitted that he, not the French, had initiated the conflict and seemed to acknowledge that Jumonville had been assassinated. "There is nothing more unworthy and lower, and even blacker, than the sentiments and the way of thinking of this Washington," a Frenchman wrote. "He lies a great deal in order to justify the assassination of Sieur Jumonville which . . . he had the stupidity to confess. . . . It would have been a pleasure to read his outrageous journal to him right under his nose."[9] A British writer mourned that Washington's signing of the articles of capitulation was "the most infamous a British subject ever put his hand to." Stung by the harsh criticism, Washington, who was inordinately sensitive to criticism and strongly blame averse, declared in his own defense, "That we were willfully, or ignorantly, deceived by our interpreter . . . I do aver, and will to my dying moment."[10]

Whatever the facts, the war had begun. Officials in London decided they could not allow the French to control the Ohio Country. Whitehall deployed two regiments of British Regulars under the command of General Edward Braddock to accomplish what Washington and his ragtag force of colonials had been unable to do. With war now inevitable, Virginia needed soldiers, and George Washington, with his military bearing, his imposing physique with persona to match, and his knack for seeming to be much older than he was, became a prime candidate for the tasks of organizing and leading Virginia's defense.

Eager to have a role in the struggle, Washington wanted to dress the part. An invoice on the eve of the war shows Washington spending fully a third of his adjutant's salary on a new dress uniform from England, including a gold shoulder knot, a hat adorned with gold lace, and the "rich crimson" coat glorious with gold braid and forty-eight gold-gilt buttons, accoutrements befitting a high-ranking Virginia officer and distinguishing him from other military personnel lacking such adornments.[11] The same invoice listed two handsome livery suits for his servants, emblazoned with his coat of arms, making it clear that he expected to ride about in high style. The lifelong attention Washington paid to his military uniforms is particularly telling, pertaining as it does to his desire to be viewed as exceptional.

Unfortunately, a dispute regarding salary and rank led to his petulant resignation. This became a pattern with young Washington. He perceived a threat to his honor or pride. Entering a world of hierarchy, posturing, and force, he was burdened with a personality sensitive to the smallest slights and lacked the seasoning to navigate around obstacles he believed others put in his path.

In the course of resigning, he declared, "My inclinations are strongly bent to arms" and implied that he remained ready to serve under the right conditions.[12] Fortunately, General Braddock's need for competent colonials familiar with the disputed region and his favorable personal impression of Washington landed Washington an informal but influential spot in the general's military "family." Washington would now share in the glory and honor that would come from driving the French out of the Ohio Valley—or so he thought. In fact, while the campaign boosted his fame, it did so in a way he could not have imagined.

Still feeling the effects of a severe bout with dysentery, Washington was riding with Braddock's forces when, on July 9, 1755, French forces and their Native American allies ambushed the British from both sides of the trail being cut near the banks of the Monongahela River, only a few miles short of their destination. The Battle of the Wilderness was one of the great British military disasters of the eighteenth century, caused in part because Braddock followed Washington's earlier advice and split his advancing army into two sections. Two-thirds of all the British officers were killed or wounded and the army routed. By all accounts, Washington conducted himself heroically. One of Washington's most salient traits was that death held no terror for him; indeed, the notion of dying heroically had a certain charm. As he later expressed it to Sally Cary Fairfax, "who is there that does not rather Envy, than regret a Death that gives birth to Honour & Glorious memory?"[13]

Absolutely fearless in battle and able to think clearly amid chaos and slaughter, Washington rallied the Virginia troops and prevented a complete rout. He carried the mortally wounded General Braddock off the field and later buried him under a wagon road to keep the victors from desecrating his remains. George Washington came very close to losing his own life as well. He was the only one of Braddock's staff officers not cut down. During the battle, he had two or three horses shot from under him, and afterward he counted four bullet holes in his clothes, one of them through his hat. In his words, "Death was levelling my companions on every side of me,"[14] but neither then nor later did a bullet ever pierce his skin, giving rise to stories among some of the Native Americans and others that he was somehow miraculously immune to gunfire. This likely convinced Washington that he enjoyed a higher power's protection. In his words, "The miraculous care of Providence . . . protected me beyond all human expectation."[15] Washington's heroic actions brought forth praise not only from fellow Virginians but from the other colonies and Britain as well.

Braddock's defeat and the hasty, almost cowardly, withdrawal of the British army into winter headquarters at Philadelphia at midsummer meant that the western frontier of Virginia, now engulfed in full-scale war, was more vulnerable to attack than ever before. A new army was needed. Once again emerging from a defeat with his reputation enhanced, George Washington was the logical choice to lead it. While declaring himself unequal to the task, at the same time he nonetheless made it clear that he would reluctantly accept command if the terms were right. This theme resurfaces in Washington's life when he is made commander in chief of the Continental Army, at the Constitutional Convention, and at his election as president. Acutely aware of appearances, he protests his inadequacy, avoids the appearance of hungering after the job, and in his seeming reluctance to take power, is able to increase the power taken. Remarkably, at the tender age of twenty-three, George Washington became the commander in chief of the armed forces of Great Britain's largest and richest colony. He was now squarely in the spotlight, although the task facing him was daunting in the extreme.

How did Washington perform? As a trainer of troops, he was excellent, and it is worth remembering that his troops were anything but the crème de la crème of Virginia. He whipped them into shape—sometimes literally whipping them and occasionally hanging malingerers as an example. In time, Washington came to believe that his Virginia Regiment was on par with the British Regulars, kept from that status only by the absence of a commission from his Royal Majesty.[16] Such validation was never forthcoming. This deeply angered the Virginia colonel, who wrote prophetically, "We cannot conceive that because we are Americans, we should therefore be deprived of the benefits common to British subjects."[17]

Frankly, Washington's job of protecting the Virginia frontier was beyond any mortal's ability. He declared, "I have been posted . . . upon our cold and Barren Frontiers, to perform I think I may say impossibilities that is, to protect from the cruel Incursions of a Crafty Savage Enemy a line of Inhabitants of more than 350 Miles extent with a force inadequate to the task."[18] Essentially, he was responsible for securing a region that was inherently indefensible, the epitome of mission impossible.

His efforts to prevail nonetheless caused him great anguish. As he wrote Governor Dinwiddie, "I am too little acquainted, Sir, with pathetic language, to attempt a description of the peoples distresses; though I have a generous soul, sensible of wrongs, and swelling for redress—But what can I do? If bleeding, dying! would glut their insatiate revenge—I would be a willing offering to Savage Fury: and die by inches, to save a people! I *see* their situation, know their danger, and participate their Sufferings; without having it in my power to give them further relief, than uncertain promises."[19]

The searing personal experiences Washington faced over these years shaped his worldview. Instead of going to college, Washington went to war. And the kind of education he received, like the smallpox he had contracted in Barbados, left scars that never went away, as well as conveying immunity against all forms of youthful idealism.[20]

Washington cannot fairly be faulted for failure to secure Virginia's frontier, but there are certainly grounds for criticizing his performance. He resigned once, threatened to resign a half dozen times, and left his men for long interludes. He seems to have employed his remarkable powers most fervently in the cause of his own self-aggrandizement. Seemingly unable to harness his ambition, in his hubris he indulged in excessive absences, petulant outbursts, and occasionally in deceitful and irresponsible conduct. He betrayed two superiors, Governor Robert Dinwiddie and General John Forbes, both of whom had his interests much at heart. His ingratitude and his treachery proceeded from an inability to comport himself according to prescriptions found in the "Rules of Civility" and the demands of honor so dear to the young warrior. His self-assertion in the quest of honor trumped his ability to show proper deference to superiors.

Washington's desire for official British army rank and his efforts to obtain it bordered on the obsessive and are best illustrated by his obsequious letter to Lord Loudoun. How different American history would have been had he achieved his goal. The young colonel, who had been promised such a position by General Braddock, now believed that his last best chance for winning a commission in the regular British army lay with Lord Loudoun, recently appointed both commander of the British forces in America and titular governor of Virginia in the summer of 1756. Washington organized a strong letter-writing campaign on his own behalf, but his initial efforts produced no breakthrough. In frustration, he complained to Dinwiddie that Loudoun had "imbibed prejudices unfavorable to my character" because he had not been "thoroughly informed."[21] Of course, the governor, as Loudoun's principal informant on affairs in Virginia, could not have avoided drawing the intended inference. His protégé was in essence accusing him of treachery.

Washington compounded his error by sending a long, shrill letter of self-justification to Loudoun. This ill-advised missive fills twelve printed pages in *The Papers of George Washington*.[22] In it, Washington blamed everyone but himself for his circumstances. He condemned local authorities for failing to track down deserters. He lambasted the assembly, where he had influential friends, for enacting "pernicious" laws and mismanaging the colony's finances. He excoriated the militia for disobedience, malingering, and waste. And he denounced the governor and the assembly for ignoring his "reiterated Letters" addressing the futility of Virginia's current military strategy. His criticism of Dinwiddie was particularly ill-advised. Not only was he bad-mouthing his own patron, the man who had advanced him as far as he could and then sponsored his further promotion, but he was doing so to his patron's patron.

Washington implied that he had not resigned earlier because of "the dawn of hope that arose" as a result of Loudoun's appointment. His obsequious letter went well beyond deference, which was proper, to servile flattery, which was not. Washington insisted on getting a chance to present his case to Loudoun in person. In time, a surprisingly tolerant Governor Dinwiddie reluctantly gave Washington permission to travel to Philadelphia, where the Virginia colonel spent six weeks early in 1757. After keeping Washington waiting for eleven days, Loudoun "dismissed George Washington with the cold, bland, impersonal courtesy of an aristocrat dealing with an inferior."[23] His dismissal meant the end of all of Washington's hopes for royal rank. And the result of his long visit to Philadelphia was more chaos on the frontier. A tension existed between self-promotion and selflessness, between personal glory and the common good. His driving ambition was proving to be a dual-edged sword, helping to propel him forward but also threatening to inflict much harm.

Colonel Washington felt he could not serve with success but neither could he resign with honor as long as Fort Duquesne remained in French hands, and capturing the fort did not seem to be a British priority in 1757. The trying situation wore on him, and, in the summer of 1757, he fell deathly ill with dysentery, or the "bloody flux," accompanied by a wracking cough, which no doubt reminded him of Lawrence's untimely demise. Eventually staggering back to Mount Vernon, where he feared a visit from "the grim king," as he once referred to death, would "certainly master my utmost efforts and that I must sink in spite of a noble struggle."[24]

Four factors coalesced to brighten his perspective. Sally Cary Fairfax came from Belvoir to nurse him. A very highly respected physician in Williamsburg assured him that his condition was not fatal. He began successfully courting the recently widowed Martha Dandridge Custis. And a new British government, now led by William Pitt, replaced the incompetent Loudoun and made the capture of Fort Duquesne a top priority. Pitt chose the highly capable General John Forbes to lead a force nearly three times the size of the army the star-crossed General Braddock had led to defeat a few years earlier.

George Washington wanted to be part of this latest expedition. Knowing a royal commission was not in the cards, he declared, "I only wish to be distinguished in some measure from the general run of provincial Officers, as I understand there will be a motley herd of us."[25] Forbes was well disposed to take advice from Washington. In only one area did Forbes spurn Washington's counsel. Washington insisted that the only way to capture Fort Duquesne in 1758 was to approach it via Braddock's Road, to the financial benefit of both Virginia and Washington, who owned land near the road. Forbes listened to Washington's arguments and decided against that track, convinced that a road moving westward across Pennsylvania was the better option.

That should have been the end of the matter, but the contentious Washington bewailed Forbes's decision to Speaker of the House John Robinson, accusing the expedition's leadership of incompetence, venality, and malfeasance. Washington's own ambition and self-interest—intimately intertwined with that of Virginia—blinded him to alternatives. Thwarted, unable to bend reality to his will, he exploded, angrily insisting that there had to be some type of corrupt bargain with Pennsylvania designed to swindle Virginia out of its rightful role as the archway to the West. "I wish," said Washington, "I was sent immediately home" (that is, to London) to denounce Forbes and promote his ideas.[26] Considering what such a journey would have cost in time and effort, the notion seems chimerical. Forbes learned of Washington's behind-the-scenes actions. "By a very unguarded letter of Col: Washington that Accidentally fell into my hands," Forbes told his second in command, "I am now at the bottom, of their Scheme against this new road, a Scheme that I think was a shame for any officer to be Concerned in."[27]

Washington feared that the general's progress west on the newly built road would be very slow, and that as a result winter would stall the British advance short of the Ohio, foreclosing his last chance at renown and honor. "That appearance of glory once in view—that laudable Ambition of Serving Our Country, and meriting its applause," he lamented, "is now no more!"[28]

George Washington was not only focused on military matters. Love and marriage were on his mind as well. The story is complicated. In September 1758, he wrote a love letter to Sally Fairfax, a letter he fervently wished that only she would read. Significantly, it was written after Washington had become engaged to Martha Custis following a brief courtship. He had ordered a ring for her from Philadelphia that June. That letter to Sally Fairfax is probably the most widely read and discussed letter that Washington ever wrote, and its meaning is still debated. There is no clear and convincing evidence that George Washington and Sally Fairfax had a sexual relationship. There is, however, clear and convincing evidence that George Washington was in love with Sally Fairfax and that she possessed strong feelings for him. Here are the letter's most salient passages:

> Tis true, I profess myself a Votary to Love [devotee to love]—I acknowledge that a Lady is in the Case—and further I confess, that this Lady is known to you,—Yes, Madam, as well as she is to one, who is too sensible of her Charms to deny the Power, whose Influence he feels and must ever Submit to. I feel the force of her amiable beauties in the recollection of a thousand tender passages that I could wish to obliterate, till I am bid to revive them—but experience alas! sadly reminds me how Impossible this is.... You have drawn me dear

> Madam, or rather I have drawn myself, into an honest confession of a Simple Fact—misconstrue not my meaning—doubt it not, nor expose it—The World has no business to know the object of my Love, declared in this manner to—you, when I want to conceal it.[29]

It should be noted that we only know of this letter because Sally kept it. Washington was not yet famous, so clearly she kept it because it meant a great deal to her. It was found with her possessions after her death and ultimately made public.

Washington admitted to being enthralled by "her charms," to the power of which he "must ever submit." He recalled "a thousand tender passages" that he might try but was unable "to obliterate." He wanted his confession kept secret: "The World has no business to know the object of my Love . . . when I want to conceal it." Are these words consistent with a playful, flirtatious letter? I think not. Whatever happened between them, the letter makes clear that Washington possessed a deep-seated capacity to feel powerful emotions.

In my view, George Washington was in love with Sally Fairfax—the wife of his friend George William Fairfax, and the daughter-in-law of his recently deceased mentor and patron, William Fairfax. Washington was on the verge of a battle he thought might claim his life, and, if he survived, on the verge of a marriage that would definitely change his life. He desperately wanted to know—did Sally also love him? Her reply, no longer extant, was vague and unsatisfactory, but it also brought Washington's life to a potential turning point. Just as his life would have changed dramatically if his mother had allowed him to join the Royal Navy, or had the British army commissioned him a regular officer, so it would have been changed had Sally encouraged him to do something romantically reckless. Happily, she did not.

Returning to military affairs, events on that front did not bear out Washington's dire predictions. Using the new road through Pennsylvania, General Forbes managed to capture the French stronghold of Fort Duquesne near the end of 1758, and without a climactic battle.

There were skirmishes, in one of which the Virginia Regiment fired on its own advance patrol, inflicting numerous deaths and casualties.[30] During the fray, Washington went among the troops, knocking up musket barrels with his sword, and much later he declared that his life had never been in more danger than at that moment. Shortly afterward, the French, undermanned, undersupplied, and facing a superior force, decided to burn and evacuate the fort, effectively ending the war in Virginia.

Though Washington achieved no great glory, he was able to return home with distinction. Despite his disappointment over Washington's actions concerning the roads, Forbes put him in charge of one of the three brigades that would lead the assault on Fort Duquesne, the only brigade entrusted to a provincial officer and clearly a high honor. The Virginia House of Burgesses voted Washington their thanks for "his faithful services to His Majesty and this Colony, and for his brave and steady behavior from the first encroachments and hostilities of the French and their Indians, to his resignation after the happy reduction of Fort Duquesne." When Washington stammered in response to their words of praise, Speaker John Robinson declared, "Sit down, Mr. Washington, your modesty equals your valor, and that surpasses the power of any language that I possess."[31]

Excerpts from the tribute his officers presented when he told them he was resigning from the service at the end of 1758 illustrate his personal impact. The officers praised Washington's "steady adherence to impartial justice, your quick Discernment and invariable Regard to Merit." They declared, "In our earliest Infancy you took us under your Tuition, trained us up in the Practice of that Discipline which alone can constitute good Troops." They bemoaned the "loss of such an excellent Commander, such a sincere Friend, and so affable a Companion. How rare it is to find those amiable Qualifications blended together in one Man? How great the loss of such a man?"[32] Reading such a tribute, it is easy to forget that the man in question was only twenty-six years old.

Martha Washington: An American Life, Michael J. Deas, 2004. (Courtesy of Michael J. Deas)

Worn out, Washington looked to an alternative, quieter future, one of domestic happiness at Mount Vernon. Barely a week after his official retirement, he married Martha Dandridge Custis on January 6, 1759. Among the many life-altering decisions George Washington made—joining Braddock's staff, accepting command of the Continental Army, attending the Constitutional Convention, accepting the presidency—I believe his marriage to Martha Custis to be the most important choice he ever made.[33]

Two reasons underpin this assertion. Following George Washington's rise to fame, one of his critics supposedly yelled out to the great man, "What would you have been if you had not married the widow Custis?" Perhaps apocryphal, that wisecrack makes a key point. Washington's remarkable success owed much to his marriage. Martha's inherited wealth catapulted him into the top echelon of Virginia's planter class and established the economic foundation for his second career as master of Mount Vernon. He could forever dispense with the servility that had sometimes marked his dealings with social betters. Martha's husband, Daniel Custis, had died suddenly in 1757, leaving no will regarding the disposition of his large fortune in slaves and land, as well as a surprising sum of liquid capital. Since he died intestate, under Virginia law one-third of his assets went directly to Martha, with the remaining two-thirds to be managed in trust for each of their two minor children, Jacky and Patsy. In modern dollars, Martha was the equivalent of a millionaire several times over.

Martha's wealth certainly appealed to George Washington. There is no question he hoped to marry a wealthy woman and had tried to do so unsuccessfully in the past. I doubt he would have pursued Martha had she not been wealthy. His initial interest was likely more economic than romantic, although Martha was both physically attractive and also had a personality capable of winning over her late husband's finicky father to champion her marriage to his son. After a very brief courtship, George and Martha wed, and Washington declared, "I am now I believe fixed at this Seat with an agreeable Consort for Life and hope to find more happiness in retirement than I ever experienced amidst a wide and bustling World."[34]

The speed of the marriage carries the whiff of a transaction.[35] Yet, however much pragmatism figured in the couple's marriage, over the years the pairing developed into a union of deep affection and love. Martha gave George Washington a gift every bit as valuable as the economic security her wealth conferred on him. That gift was psychological security. She gave Washington the unconditional support and love that his personality, perhaps due to his difficult childhood, seemed to yearn for. This support was essential to his eventual success. Indeed, one could argue that their marriage was "the most successful and consequential [union] in American History."[36]

With an agreeable consort and control over a large fortune, George Washington was ready to begin a new chapter in his life. That chapter would turn out very differently than he could have possibly imagined in 1759.

3

FROM LOYAL VIRGINIA GENTLEMAN TO REBEL CHIEFTAIN

1759–1775

WITH HIS RESIGNATION FROM command of the First Virginia Regiment and his marriage to Martha Custis, George Washington entered a new chapter in his life. His lifestyle changed dramatically, but his personality did not. His ambition, energy, competitiveness, passion, and drive remained as strong as ever but now were to be channeled differently. He now would focus his relentless pursuit of distinction in three intertwining arenas: the social, the political, and the economic. By 1775, Washington had succeeded in all three areas. In addition, he had evolved into the "complete gentleman" he had long sought to become, a status seemingly out of reach in 1758. If, during the first two stages of his life, he had been a "man on the make," by 1775 he was clearly a man who had made it.

Conscious of what he called his "defective education" (untrained in language or the classics),[1] he applied himself to polishing his communication skills. For this rigorous student in the school of self-improvement, the results were tangible. His grasp of the written word, including handwriting, grammar, and organization, improved significantly between 1759 and 1775. Part of that improvement came

The West Front of Mount Vernon, Edward Savage, ca. 1787–92. (Mount Vernon Ladies' Association)

from spending many a quiet hour in his study at Mount Vernon simply reading, and he read much more than is generally recognized.[2] A life-long news junkie, he perused weekly papers, especially the *Virginia Gazette,* for up-to-date information on business and politics.

During the years before the Revolution, the master of Mount Vernon led a life of supercharged sociability. "Amiable," a label often applied to Washington while he lived, saw much less use in the years following his death. He enjoyed the gift of complaisance, that is, an ability to make oneself agreeable to others and a characteristic central to being a gentleman. "Good Breeding," wrote John Locke, "has no other use or end, but to make People easy and satisfied in their conversation with us."[3] Historians have not given enough attention to Washington's "soft side," especially the sociability that was central to his personality before 1775 and crucial to his success after 1775.

Most of Washington's recreational activities were social in nature and typical of his time, place, and class. We tend to forget that he experienced a healthy enjoyment of worldly pleasures, and manifested no zeal for self-denial. The familiar image of the cold, self-sacrificing altruist does not properly apply to George Washington. He loved to dance, charmed women, and he enjoyed good conversation over long, leisurely dinners enhanced by glasses of Madeira. He entertained and was entertained, almost nonstop. Between 1768 and 1775, for example, he and Martha received approximately two thousand guests at Mount Vernon. He went to horse races, boat races, and barbecues. He played at billiards, backgammon, and cards—in the last category meticulously recording his winnings and losses. He hunted and fished. He danced at balls and attended the theater. Indeed, he went to the theater at every opportunity, eventually attending more than a hundred productions. Over time, he would come to see himself as playing a special role on history's stage, and he benefited in that role from watching professional actors exhibit their skills.

The sport that Washington favored above all others was fox hunting. He rode to the hounds spring, summer, fall, and winter—especially during the winter, when the responsibilities of farming and public service were at their least. In January and February 1768, he "went a fox hunting" fourteen or fifteen times and would have been on the chase more often but for bad weather.

Fox hunting must have gratified Washington on many levels, conscious and subconscious. It provided an outlet for his enormous reserves of energy, and, calling as it does on all the body's parts, riding competitively kept him physically fit. Leaping ditches, streams, and fences at full gallop on a horse that he had bred and trained while clad in striking garments that he ordered from Great Britain no doubt imbued him with the feeling of well-being associated with skillfully performing a challenging activity before an appreciative audience. Washington became acknowledged as the finest horseman in Virginia, a prestigious title indeed.

The George Washington of this period was not all stoic gravitas but rather a much friendlier and more approachable companion than the stiff, aloof figure of legend. He enjoyed people and had many friends,

View of Mount Vernon with the Washington Family on the Piazza, Benjamin Henry Latrobe, 1796. (Mount Vernon Ladies' Association)

among them Robert Orme, Dr. James Craik, Burwell Bassett, John Posey, Captain Robert Stewart, and Jack, his favorite brother. His ability to make himself agreeable to others helps explain his charismatic appeal to contemporaries as well as his superlative leadership ability.

These qualities undoubtedly enhanced his success politically as well as socially. While Washington fostered an image of himself as "disinterested" in advancing his position in the realm of politics, a re-examination of his career, focusing on his political activities, indicates perpetual interest and involvement in that arena throughout his adult life.[4] Such study reveals him to have been a political operator both ambitious and astute. For instance, he collected and saved the poll lists from each of the contested elections in which he ran for the House of Burgesses, even keeping one roster from a race involving his half brother Lawrence. Furthermore, he took the trouble to alphabetize the contents of some of those lists, evidently to enhance their utility during future races. At the age of twenty-three, in another example of Washington's youthful audacity, he had his brother Jack secretly test the waters in Fairfax County to see if he might be able to run for a seat in the House of Burgesses despite the fact that he held no local offices at the time. There was no such opening.

After another false start the same year in Frederick County, in 1758 George Washington, at age twenty-six, won election to the House of Burgesses from that county, and in doing so spent an inordinate amount of money to "treat" the voters to alcoholic refreshment. Washington paid £39 out of his own pocket for 160 gallons of beer, wine, rum, punch, and cider—roughly half a gallon of spirits for each vote he received.[5] And he wondered whether that was enough!

Three years later, in one of the less admirable acts of his life, he urged the sheriff of Frederick County to bend election law. Most likely his goal was to assist in the reelection of his fellow candidate George Mercer, who was facing a challenge from Washington's former military subordinate Colonel Adam Stephen. "I hope and indeed make no doubt," Washington wrote, "that you will contribute your aid towards shutting [Stephen] out of the Public trust he is seeking, could Mercer's Friends and mine be hurried in at the first of the Poll it might be an advantage." He quickly noted that as sheriff, "I know you cannot appear in this, nor would I by any mean have you do anything that can give so designing a Man as Colo. Stevens the least trouble."[6] Of course, that was exactly what Washington was asking the sheriff to do. In 1765, he won election as Fairfax County's representative in the House of Burgesses, a seat he held basically without opposition until the coming of the war.

Washington became increasingly active at the community level as well. He was a vestryman for Truro Parish, a justice of the peace for Fairfax County, and a trustee for the city of Alexandria. His papers reveal a man with a growing sense of civic responsibility and a man of considerable generosity to family, friends, and the community at large. An excellent example is Washington's willingness to help the son of his friend William Ramsay attend Princeton College. "No other return is expected or wished for," he assured Ramsay, "than that you will accept it with the same freedom & good will with which it is made."[7]

This philanthropy and the hope that William's education would "not only promote his own happiness, but the future welfare of others" was emblematic of Washington's enlightened gentility. He was pragmatic, progressive, benevolent, and cosmopolitan. He also served as executor for numerous neighbors' estates. Washington's rendering of service to his neighbors daily increased his sense of obligation to them and, at the same time, deepened his patience with and understanding of his fellow man. Much of his charitable giving was done anonymously so it is not possible to ascertain its full extent.

Awareness of George Washington's growing sense of noblesse oblige and community service should not lead one to conclude that he disregarded his own economic interests. He certainly desired to stand out in this sphere too. Wealth meant autonomy and independence, both vital to Washington, who strongly desired to be in control of his life. It is impossible to read his personal papers and not come away with a profound sense of how powerfully Washington strove to enhance his wealth. He was a crafty and diligent entrepreneur, excessively and conspicuously assiduous in the defense of his own interests. In multiple commercial contexts he habitually measured time, distance, and quantity, always with an eye to cost and benefit. He was constantly, one might say obsessively, calculating virtually every aspect of all the various revenue-producing operations going on at Mount Vernon. For example, he checked to see how many shirts were completed by a seamstress while monitored as opposed to not being monitored.

The master of Mount Vernon had two main financial concerns—to make his plantations profitable and to assure the profitability of his large investments in Western lands. He managed to double the acreage of Mount Vernon to about 6,500 acres (and eventually to approximately 8,000 acres); greatly increased his enslaved work force (ultimately to over three hundred souls); switched his Mount Vernon farms from growing tobacco to raising more profitable grains; started a moneymaking milling enterprise; engaged in a profitable fisheries business; and traded extensively in the Caribbean, even becoming a ship owner. Later he ran a profitable distillery. He used—critics with some justification would say misused—his service in the French and Indian War as a springboard to finally acquiring what would add up to over 33,000 acres of land west of the Alleghenies. Much of that acreage was, in his words, "the cream of the country,"[8] to which Washington argued he was entitled because without his efforts those holdings would never have become available to the veterans of the war in the first place.

While, in time, Washington would grow increasingly concerned about the institution of slavery and would in his final will and testament outline a program to free all of his enslaved workers, there is sadly little evidence during this period of his life that he was anything other than a typical Virginia planter.[9] (Washington's attitude toward slavery is examined in the afterword to this volume.)

By 1775, George Washington had clearly succeeded in his second career as master of Mount Vernon. Triumphant at many levels and a planter of the first rank, he had evolved into the "complete gentleman" that he had long wished to be. Why would such a man—successful, wealthy, and essentially conservative—be willing to become, in the words of a British critic, a "rebel chieftain," leading an armed resistance against what Washington had earlier referred to as "my king and country"?

Certainly, in 1758, the idea that he would lead a revolt of the American colonies against the British Empire would have seemed preposterous to George Washington. He was British in culture; he admired England and modeled his own lifestyle on that of the English gentry. Yet, over time, his view of Great Britain soured, and the radical Whig image of a corrupt, power-hungry ministry became more and more resonant and believable to him. While complicated and multifarious, this transformation beckons for a closer historical review.

The early 1700s saw a surge of aggressive nationalism in Great Britain. By midcentury, Britons were more emphatically defining colonial Americans as "others," a separate people, geographically remote, and not fully English.[10] For colonists like Washington, ever striving for membership in that exclusive club, and yet ever thwarted in said pursuit, the realization that the British regarded white colonial Americans as second-class beings came as a frustrating shock. Washington first experienced this bias in the French and Indian War. He believed that Americans of high achievement were no less deserving than Englishmen of high station. "We can't conceive," he wrote, "that being Americans should deprive us of the benefits of British Subjects."[11] His inability to win a royal commission, try as he might, undoubtedly gnawed at him.

Great Britain disappointed George Washington in ways beyond his quixotic quest for military rank. In his business pursuits, Washington soon ran into difficulties with British merchants and policies that parallel his stunted alliance with the British army. In commerce, Washington was a highly capable and disciplined businessman and an advanced "scientific" farmer, but he found his efforts constantly thwarted by policies and actions of Great Britain and its merchants that seemed increasingly not only shortsighted but mean-spirited as well.[12]

Washington's correspondence with his agent Robert Cary amounts to a litany of complaints about the low prices his tobacco brought—the Custis plantations produced about 100,000 pounds of tobacco a year during the 1760s—and the high prices charged him for shoddy and outdated imported products. He felt that he was being discriminated against simply because he was an American and because people like Cary believed he did not deserve first-class treatment. The situation worsened when Washington found himself ever-deeper in debt. His towering ego balked at the realization that his very fate was in the hands of British creditors an ocean away, whom he believed to be manipulating interest rates in a massive imperial swindle. The whole mercantile system, embodied by Robert Cary, seemed designed to foster dependency, and if there was anything the master of Mount Vernon wished to avoid, it was a sense of dependency.[13] His treatment at the hands of London traders only strengthened his tendency to think of himself as an American.

Earlier, and with much more clarity than most others, Washington saw that the future of America—and the way to great personal fortune—lay in the huge untapped resources of the regions west of the Allegheny Mountains. Washington's dream of a landed independence and American expansion kept clashing with the reality of imperial policy. Here, as in his quest for a British commission and for success as a tobacco planter, he found himself thwarted by what he viewed as unjust actions by Great Britain's Parliament and leaders. First the Proclamation Act of 1763 sought to close the vast regions west of the Alleghenies to Anglo-American settlers. Then, in the so-called "Intolerable Acts" of 1774, Parliament unceremoniously detached from Virginia the land north of the Ohio River, assigning jurisdiction over that huge parcel to Canada. That action created unfavorable conditions for the development of Washington's large tract on the Great Kanawha River. As a crowning blow, on March 21, 1775, Virginia's governor, Lord Dunmore, suddenly canceled Washington's claim to thousands of acres of prime land—apparently on the pretext that Washington's surveyor, William Crawford, was not qualified and properly licensed to make the pertinent surveys.[14]

Hopefully, the picture sketched above makes George Washington's decisions more understandable. An intensely ambitious man, he found his initial undertakings blocked and himself treated as a second-class citizen. Denied official British rank, hampered in his efforts to prosper as a tobacco planter, thwarted in his dream of a Western empire, George Washington was understandably receptive to an ideology that railed against corruption and tyranny.

And the radical Whig message was not only negative. The Whig philosophy also held out the promise of virtuous, liberty-loving freemen enjoying lives of independence and advancing as far as their individual talents could take them. Perchance in joining and supporting this new ideology, George Washington saw both a promising cause and the chance to achieve his long-held desire for fame and glory.

A reluctant revolutionary concerning full independence, Washington always insisted on what he viewed as his individual rights, and from quite early on he was willing, if need be, to take up arms to protect those rights. His most famous statement in this vein is a 1769 letter to his neighbor and early mentor George Mason: "At a time when our lordly Masters in Great Britain will be satisfied with nothing less than the deprivation of American freedom, it seems highly necessary that something shou'd be done to avert the stroke and maintain the liberty which we have derived from our Ancestors; . . . That no man shou'd scruple, or hesitate a moment to use a-ms [Washington could not write out the emotive word "arms" in its entirety but instead wrote *a*, dash, *ms*] in defense of so valuable a blessing, on which all the good and evil of life depends; is clearly my opinion."[15] A much less well-known letter from Arthur Lee makes clear that Washington was willing to fight as early as 1768 if the situation demanded it.[16]

Washington became increasingly convinced that the possibility of armed conflict loomed because of Britain's continuing abuses. As he wrote in 1774 to his good friend, Tory-leaning Bryan Fairfax, "The crisis is arrived when we must assert our rights, or submit to every imposition that can be heaped upon us; till custom and use, will make us as tame, and abject slaves as the blacks we rule over with such arbitrary sway."[17]

The ministry persisted, and blood flowed at Lexington and Concord in April 1775, just as Washington had feared it would. "Unhappy it is though to reflect, that a Brother's sword has been sheathed in a Brother's breast," he wrote, "and that, the once happy and peaceful plains of America are either to be drenched with blood or inhabited by slaves. Sad alternative! But can a virtuous man hesitate in his choice?"[18] Even before the fighting erupted, Washington informed his brother Jack that, if necessary, he was fully prepared to "devote my life and fortune" to the cause of resisting British oppression.[19] Now, in the aftermath of Lexington and Concord, George Washington, as a virtuous man, had made his choice. Arms might have been the last resort, but the time for arms had come.

With the outbreak of the fighting at Lexington and Concord, the Second Continental Congress, meeting in Philadelphia, recognized that it had to raise a Continental army and make the crucially important decision of choosing a commander for that force. The traditional version of what happened next is well known. John Adams nominated a reluctant George Washington to lead the yet-to-be-raised Continental army. Upon hearing the beginning of Adams's speech, a surprised and embarrassed Washington bolted from the room and encouraged his friend and attorney Edmund Pendleton to oppose the nomination. He then emphasized to his fellow delegates that he had not sought the nomination and did not think himself capable of doing the job. This account garbles the true dynamics at play. Since commanding the Continental Army most shaped Washington's place in history, the mechanics behind that decision merit scrutiny.

From the beginning, Washington was the leading candidate to lead the rebel army, and, with the advantage of historical hindsight, one might deem his appointment inevitable. Not by chance was he unanimously chosen. There are several reasons for these assumptions.

George Washington had an excellent reputation in New England, based on his service in the French and Indian War. He was the only congressional delegate with significant fighting experience and the leading soldier from the largest North American colony. Virginia always commanded attention. Significantly, six counties from all geographical areas of the colony—Fairfax, Prince William, Albemarle, Spotsylvania, Richmond, and Westmoreland—had chosen Washington to command their independent companies. In his home county of Fairfax, he and George Mason designed the militia's buff-and-blue uniforms, later to be adopted for the officers of the new American army. The two men made Fairfax County a leader in the resistance movement through innovative actions, including levying a "voluntary" tax to underwrite the militia.

The congressional delegates widely, if inaccurately, believed that following the passage of the Intolerable Acts in 1774, Washington had offered to raise and train one thousand men and send them to Boston's aid at his own expense.[20] As he was passing through Baltimore while making his way to Philadelphia in May 1775, Baltimoreans feted Washington as an expert military man and asked him to review their volunteer units. His arrival in Philadelphia drew a turnout unmatched by any other delegate.

Congress immediately put him on four important military committees, including panels assigned to find ways to defend New York City, secure ammunition and supplies for the coming conflict, and organize the troops. Washington's chairmanship of these committees gave leading delegates from nearly every colony the opportunity to work with him. Looking to him for soldierly advice, they also took the measure of the man and liked what they saw.

Politically, visually, and in terms of character, Washington was virtually the ideal choice. Certainly, there were "political" considerations to take into account. Virginia was by far the largest, most populous, and wealthiest of the thirteen colonies, and New England leaders desired and needed Virginia's support and active participation in the upcoming struggle. Had Washington hailed from Delaware, he might not have been chosen. But being a Virginian, though significant, was not sufficient. Other factors were also important. Compared with the run of native-born Americans, he had significant military experience. At the age of forty-three he was mature but still very vigorous and in the prime of his manhood.

Equally important, George Washington looked the part. His military air and bearing, augmented by the wearing of his brand-new uniform, impressed virtually everyone. "He has so much martial dignity in his deportment," wrote Dr. Benjamin Rush of Philadelphia, "that you would distinguish him to be a general and a soldier from among ten thousand people. There is not a king in Europe that would not look like a *valet de chambre* by his side."[21]

Even more important, George Washington was the type of leader in whom American Patriots could take great pride. A devoted family man of great wealth and moderate views, he was nevertheless fully committed to the Patriot cause. Washington's character and demeanor clearly impressed his fellow delegates, and that appeal only grew with more exposure. As delegate Silas Deane expressed it, "The more I am acquainted with, the more I esteem him. . . . His Virtues do not shine in the View of the World by reason of his great Modesty but when discovered by the discerning Eye, shine proportionally brighter."[22] Massachusetts delegate Thomas Cushing succinctly summarized George Washington's character: "He is a complete gentleman. He is sensible, amiable, virtuous, modest, and brave."[23] George Washington combined in an exceptional fashion the courtesy and complaisance of a courtier with the appearance and record of a warrior. This compelling blend of diffidence and power made him attractive to many and acceptable to all.[24]

How did Washington feel about these developments? Did he want the appointment? Both publicly and privately, he denied any such desire. Perhaps we can come closest to understanding Washington's expressed perspective by considering words he wrote his wife, Martha, in one of the very rare such letters to survive: "I have used every endeavor in my power to avoid it, not only from my unwillingness to part with you and the family, but from a consciousness of its being a trust too great for my capacity, and that I should enjoy more real happiness in one month with you at home, than I have the most distant prospect of finding abroad, if my stay were to be seven times seven years."[25]

While containing much truth, this representation fails to accurately tell the complete story. Although impossible to definitively prove, the accumulated evidence indicates that George Washington wanted the position and worked to make it very likely that it would be offered to him.

There is no disputing his desire for military glory in the French and Indian War. Even near the end of that frightful conflict, he was endorsing the benefits of a heroic death. Remember that he wrote Sally Fairfax, "who is there that does not rather Envy, than regret a Death that gives birth to Honour & Glorious memory?"[26] Even after the war, it is worth noting that he tried—unsuccessfully as it turned out—to buy for display at Mount Vernon busts of renowned military figures, including graven images of Julius Caesar, Alexander the Great, and Frederick the Great. He also ordered statuary showing "2 furious wild beasts of any kind," posed "as if approaching each other and eager to engage," a warlike image indeed. The painters of the Enlightenment celebrated a virtuous death as man's greatest triumph, and Washington had several such paintings hanging in his Mount Vernon home. In 1772, he prepared to have his portrait painted by Charles Willson Peale. Significantly, as most likely he thought this would be the only portrait of him, he donned his old uniform from the French and Indian War, now fourteen years in the past. He wanted to be remembered as a soldier.

Before departing Mount Vernon for the Second Continental Congress, he had visits from both Horatio Gates and Charles Lee, comrades-in-arms from the French and Indian War and former British officers, who no doubt wondered what place, if war came, they could find in the armed forces of the colonies, which they had resolved to support. Certainly, George Washington entertained the same thoughts. He was simply too smart and too ambitious not to do so.

And, of course, George Washington donned his military uniform while attending the sessions of Congress. There has been some dispute as to which military uniform he wore, but it now seems clear that it was the new buff-and-blue uniform he had designed for the Fairfax County militia. The Italians have a phrase—*una bella figura*—that sums up the perfect gesture made in the perfect way. Washington arriving at Independence Hall in buff and blue was *una bella figura* if ever there was one. And, of all the members attending Congress, as far as we know, only he appeared in uniform. When you are over six feet tall, of imposing martial bearing, and wearing a brand-new uniform when you know there is virtual unanimity among the delegates that an army is to be formed, it can't come as a total shock to discover that you are being seriously considered for the position.

General George Washington at Trenton, John Trumbull, 1792. (Yale University Art Gallery; gift of the Society of the Cincinnati)

Isn't this an effective gesture? On one level, wearing the uniform wordlessly exhibited his commitment to American rights, meanwhile signaling his availability and tacitly invoking his military experience. No one made him wear his uniform day after day to chair four key military committees as Congress was preparing for war. One scholar has compared Washington wearing his uniform to Congress to a party guest bringing along a guitar, unsubtly telegraphing a wish to be asked to play.[27] Of course, Washington did not lobby for the position. That would have triggered Whiggish fears of power. Washington shaped his public performance to match the Whig "Country Party" beliefs and ideals, notably its belief in the perils of power and its tendency to expand and corrupt those who hold it.

It is not accurate to say Washington did everything he could to keep from being appointed. His surviving letter to Martha makes explicit that he knew he was seriously being considered for some time prior to his actual nomination. Significantly, despite that fact, he did little if anything to discourage such talk. For example, he might have proposed another candidate for the position, but it is clear that he did not do so. In chairing four key military committees at the very time Congress was recognizing the need for a Continental army, he highlighted his qualifications. At one level he must have known that no other American was more qualified than he to lead the army of the united colonies. If he truly wanted to defend American liberty, he could make but one decision.[28]

In *Julius Caesar*, William Shakespeare observes, "There is a tide in the affairs of men, which taken at the flood, leads on to fortune."[29] There are certain key moments in a person's life, and success most likely comes when a person can create or simply recognize and act upon such moments. George Washington created those moments in the French and Indian War and in his marriage to Martha Washington. Now he was helping to create what turned out to be the most significant moment in his life as a historical figure.

Washington had a deep and burning desire for fame and glory. His rekindling dream of military glory, his political commitments, and his continued striving for public recognition all now coincided and opened onto the more expansive vista of a greater honor. The yearning for esteem became a quest for historical immortality.

This would be difficult for Washington to verbalize or even consciously recognize. The forces that drive human activities are very complicated. Washington understood that when he wrote a close friend, "we know little of ourselves."[30] John Adams later wrote, George

Washington "did not know his own heart . . . he did not know himself" when it came to such questions.[31] In responding to the call of duty, there was always hidden desire.[32] My colleague Joseph Ellis is correct when he argues that Washington had considerable trouble acknowledging his own ambitions: "His claim that he had no interest in the commander-in-chief post was not so much a lie as an essential fabrication that shielded him from the recognition that, within a Continental Congress filled with ambitious men, he was the most ambitious—not just the tallest—man in the room."[33]

On the other hand, it is also clear that Washington's abiding hunger for recognition battled a genuine sense of trepidation at the magnitude of the task ahead. While eager for the position, he feared failure. His appointment as commander in chief both gratified and terrified a man who was such a mix of confidence and insecurity.[34]

Failure to achieve his mission—and think of the difficulty of that mission—would cost him his dearly desired reputation, and quite likely his life. Yet the chance to lead America in what soon became the "glorious cause," to defend and strengthen liberty and republicanism, and to earn glory and fame for George Washington was a "win-win" situation. He wanted the position and acted in a manner to win it, but he did so with subtlety and wisdom.

Demonstrating modesty, which was as much a part of his character as courage, he did not curry favor in the manner of a politician, nor did he promise triumph as many a military man might. He spoke as an honest man would speak to friends, confessing his hopes and fears.[35] And then, in stark contrast to the corruption and self-dealing of the British imperial order, he refused to be paid for the sacrifices he was about to make. This refusal won particular praise. By offering to serve without pay, George Washington went far to demonstrate that he could be trusted with power because he took it reluctantly, would not abuse it, and would relinquish it when the mission was done. Essentially, he fashioned a public mask of extraordinary virtue which he would wear for the rest of his life.[36]

It should be emphasized that while Washington desired fame and glory, he was not after fame and glory won by amassing great power. He rightly declared, "I have no lust for power."[37] Rather his glory was to be obtained by serving the greater good, a service which would earn him the affection and admiration of his fellow men that he so desperately desired.

Provided, of course, that he could carry out the mission successfully. The task was daunting in the extreme. Success had to seem a very long shot indeed. Shortly after being nominated, Washington spoke with Patrick Henry and told that great rebel to remember his words that, with this nomination, "I date the fall and ruin of my reputation."[38] Happily for George Washington, and for the country he came to love and to father, he could not have been more mistaken.

4

AMERICA'S CINCINNATUS

1775–1783

THE FOURTH CHAPTER OF George Washington's life began with his appointment on June 15, 1775, as commander in chief of the yet-to-be organized Continental army. It would prove to be the most challenging period of his life, and that is saying something.

One key to Washington's success was the remarkable extent to which he observed, grasped, and fulfilled his countrymen's expectations. A wonderful example of this is his refusal to accept any payment for his services beyond reimbursement for expenses. This quiet symbolic gesture, one of the more important acts of Washington's entire career, deeply impressed the populace he served. One of Washington's greatest talents was his ability to win the confidence and trust of others. He assured fellow citizens that "when we assumed the Soldier, we did not lay aside the citizen, and we shall most sincerely rejoice with you in that happy hour, when the establishment of American liberty . . . shall enable us to return to our Private stations in the bosom of a free, peaceful & happy Country."[1]

His stance soon generated comparisons to the fifth-century BCE Roman statesman Cincinnatus, who decamped from his estate to put

The Passage of the Delaware, Thomas Sully, 1819. (Photograph © 2025 Museum of Fine Arts, Boston)

down a threat to the republic and, having achieved that goal, gave up power and returned to private life. John Adams expressed the appeal Washington exerted on so many Americans: "A gentleman of one of the first fortunes on the continent, leaving his delicious retirement, his family and friends, sacrificing his ease, and hazarding all in the cause of his country."[2]

Understanding the power of imagery, immediately after his appointment Washington paid a Philadelphia tailor £12 to stitch up a regimental uniform of better workmanship, materials, and trimmings than one fashioned recently but with significantly less skill by Mount Vernon's indentured tailor, Andrew Judge.[3] To complement his new uniform Washington then ordered a "blue ribband" to "distinguish myself." He certainly looked the part of an American hero, and, frankly, that look was one reason for his success. A typical statement by Dr. James Thacher in 1778 indicates Washington's charismatic appeal:

"The serenity of his countenance, and majestic gracefulness of his deportment, impart a strong impression of that dignity and grandeur, which are his peculiar characteristics, and no one can stand in his presence without feeling the ascendancy of his mind, and associating with his countenance the idea of wisdom, philanthropy, magnanimity, and patriotism."[4]

While Washington might have projected the appearance of being primed for victory, his arrival to the area outside of Boston drove home the epic nature of the challenge he faced. His military force could hardly be called an army. Chaos seemed to reign. Soldiers of the era customarily went into battle with forty musket rounds and enough powder to fire them. To Washington's shock, he could issue only nine rounds per man. As an aristocrat reared in a culture of deference, Washington chafed at New Englanders' overly democratic ways, such as their willingness to erase the social barriers between gentlemen and plebians and to allow regular soldiers to elect their own officers. Washington soon wrote a friend in Virginia that the New Englanders were "the most indifferent kind of people I ever saw . . . an exceeding dirty and nasty people."[5] To his chagrin, these and other slurs from his private letters reached the popular press, quickly teaching him to mind his manners.

Space limitations dictate an episodic approach to this account, which will focus on the way General Washington approached the war, his philosophy, some of the challenges he faced, and why he succeeded.

General Washington wrote a particularly revealing letter to Lund Washington, his cousin, to whom he had delegated the management of Mount Vernon in his absence. The date was September 30, 1776. That March, Washington had successfully forced the British to evacuate Boston. For that achievement, Congress voted to give him a gold medal, but his fortunes quickly went downhill. Tasked with protecting New York City, Washington's overmatched army was trounced in the Battle of Long Island in late August. He and his troops narrowly escaped to New York City. Two weeks later the foe humiliated Washington's forces at the Battle of Kips Bay in Lower Manhattan. Unable to rally his men,

Washington lamented, "Are these the troops with which I am to protect America?" One of his closest aides, Tench Tilghman, left a vivid image of the General and his state of mind: "He snapped his pistols . . . three times dashed his hat to the ground, and at last exclaimed 'Good God have I got such troops as those' . . . [W]ithin 80 yards of the enemy, [he was] so vexed at the infamous conduct of his troops that he sought death rather life."[6] Fortunately, aides led him off the field to live and fight another day.

It was against this backdrop that a beleaguered Washington wrote to cousin Lund, revealing his anguish:

> Such is my situation that if I were to wish the bitterest curse to an enemy on this side of the grave, I should put him in my stead with my feelings; and yet I do not know what plan of conduct to pursue. I see the impossibility of serving with reputation, or doing any essential service to the cause by continuing in command, and yet I am told that if I quit the command inevitable ruin will follow from the distraction that will ensue. In confidence I tell you that I never was in such an unhappy, divided state since I was born. To lose all comfort and happiness on the one hand, whilst I am fully persuaded that under such a system of management as has been adopted, I cannot have the least chance for reputation, . . . and to be told, on the other, that if I leave the service all will be lost, is, at the same time that I am bereft of every peaceful moment, distressing to a degree.[7]

The letter illustrates both Washington's compulsion to safeguard his reputation and also his fear of disgrace, a lifelong refrain. Indeed, while ordering his cousin not to make the missive's contents public for fear of damaging the cause, Washington gave Lund permission to do so posthumously: "If I fall, it may not be amiss that these circumstances be known, and declaration made in credit to the justice of my character."[8] He did not want the world blaming him for not being able to accomplish the impossible.

The letter hints at the tremendous sacrifices Washington was making for his new country, a theme he expounded on later that year, writing to his brother Samuel, "You can form no Idea of the perplexity of my Situation. No Man, I believe, ever had a greater choice of difficulties and less means to extricate himself from them."[9] Of course, the war continued for over eight long years, and the problems just kept coming. The General groaned that his life was "one continued round of annoyance and fatigue."[10] His mind, he declared, "was constantly on the stretch."[11] He described himself as "a man who is daily injuring his private estate without even the smallest earthly advantage."[12]

William Ferraro, editor of volume 34 in the *Revolutionary War Series* of *The Papers of George Washington,* has highlighted the stress endured by His Excellency, as Washington was called, during the Yorktown Campaign: "What a full engagement with the documentary record reveals is a much more fretful, divisive, and racially-charged environment through this period than conveyed in the standard triumphalist accounts. There is evidence . . . of GW actually being on the point of cracking."[13]

The existence of so much material from the war—thirty-four thick volumes and counting—is strictly due to Washington himself and the actions he took. Amid severe financial constraints, the General convinced Congress to hire writers to work "under the inspection of a man of character in whom entire confidence can be placed . . . for the sole purpose of recording the voluminous papers that were generated by the war."[14] Several men needed in excess of two years to complete this task. Whenever the undertaking and its staff had to relocate, His Excellency ordered, "the wagons should never be without a sentinel over them; always locked and the key in your possession."[15] Washington explicitly stated that his papers, which he said had much value for him, "undoubtedly will claim the attention of the Historian." No one was more earnest than George Washington in courting posterity.

To be plunged into an endless sequence of war, controversy, and crisis, walking the knife edge of catastrophe, must have been grim indeed.[16] While a myriad of difficulties might have brought him close to the breaking point, in fact he never cracked. His steely determination is one of the key pillars of his personality, and he always showed remarkable persistence in the face of severe adversity, including an effort by some officers and congressmen to replace him as commander in chief in an incident known as the Conway Cabal. As Robert Morris, the financier of the American Revolution, noted, Washington "feeds and thrives on misfortune by finding resources to get the better of them," whereas lesser leaders "sink under their weight, thinking it impossible to succeed."[17]

Washington didn't know whether he would succeed, but he would do his damnedest. His favorite play was *Cato* by Joseph Addison, and one of Addison's best lines—lines which Washington quoted in correspondence at least three different times—was, "It is not in the power of man to command [assure] success. We will do more, Sempronius. We will deserve it."[18] George Washington strove always to deserve success, and even his critics acknowledged that he could not be bribed, corrupted, or compromised.[19]

George Washington not only embodied integrity and displayed an unwavering support for the cause, he brought to the war a mind that was perfectly suited to a commander's executive and administrative responsibilities.[20] Not intellectually brilliant in the way of Jefferson or Hamilton or Franklin, Washington nonetheless had a powerful and capacious mind. His wartime writings reveal an impressive mentality able to aggregate and retain information on widely divergent topics and shift nimbly among complex subjects—strategic planning, military intelligence, logistics, disputes regarding rank, recruitment, management of prisoners, interactions with Congress, finance, diplomacy, America's multifaceted relationship with France, etc. He had a powerful memory, an appetite for information, and an ability to digest and categorize mounds of facts so that those data could be of meaningful use—all while leading an army in the field. It is difficult to imagine anyone else in the country capable of doing that towering job nearly as well.

Four disparate topics illuminate Washington's philosophy and character as he struggled to lead America to victory over Great Britain: his call for a professional army, his goal of winning the "hearts and minds" of America's citizens, his firm belief in civilian control of the military, and his actions in combat at Trenton and Princeton.

In that long September 1776 letter to cousin Lund, Washington singled out as the reason he had "the least chance for reputation" the refusal by Congress to create a standing army with stipulated and lengthy enlistment periods. To understand Washington's view as the commanding general, it is important to recognize that he passionately believed the Patriots had to establish a professional army based on the British model and to keep that army in the field until the enemy despaired of achieving victory. A persistent popular myth of the Revolution then and now is that God-fearing, patriotic, and brave citizens could defeat the British army and its foreign hirelings. In this fantasy, citizen soldiers, imbued with virtue and motivated by love of country and good intentions, would overcome the professional redcoats and mercenaries deployed to force the rebellious colonies back into line.

General Washington did not subscribe to that view. He knew that revolutionary fervor could go only so far. Virtue alone was too shaky a foundation upon which to construct a republican army. It always had to be tied to interest, because he believed that "the motives which predominate most in human affairs [are] self-love and self-interest."[21] Washington championed the creation of a professional army. He grasped, as most of his countrymen did not, that only a standing army of professional veterans stood a chance of winning independence. Of course, this posed a chronic problem. A standing army "violated the very principles the American Revolution purportedly embodied," wrote Joseph Ellis. "Yet, while a standing army might be an anathema to republican principles, it was the only way to win the war. And defeat rendered all the republican principles irrelevant."[22]

His Excellency sought to make his case to Congress: "The Jealousies of a standing Army, and the Evils to be apprehended from one, are remote; and in my judgment, situated and circumstanced as we are, not at all to be dreaded. . . . I am persuaded and as fully convinced as I am of any fact . . . that our liberties must of necessity be greatly hazarded, if not entirely lost if their defense is left to any but a permanent standing army."[23]

From his earliest experiences in uniform, Washington had learned to distrust militias, which were irregular bodies of haphazardly trained troops led by amateur officers, with all ranks from the same locality, and contracted to serve for limited periods. Militiamen might annoy and inflict casualties on the British army, but they simply lacked the military capability to remove the king's men, and the British had more than enough resources to outlast such operations as state militias could undertake.

While Washington learned to use the militia with some effectiveness, he always doubted their value: "To place any dependence upon Militia, is, assuredly, resting upon a broken staff."[24] Why? "Militia, who come in, you cannot tell how—go, you cannot tell when—and act, you cannot tell where—consume your provisions—exhaust your Stores, and leave you at last at a critical moment."[25] His conclusion: "If I was called upon to declare upon Oath, whether the Militia have been most serviceable or hurtful upon the whole; I should subscribe to the latter."

A second important aspect in understanding George Washington as commander in chief is that while he did not use the phrase "hearts and minds," he very early recognized that winning the war depended on winning fellow Americans' hearts and minds. He had to convince American skeptics to trust that the army would behave as good republicans. His advice to officers distilled his view: "Discourage vice in every shape, and impress upon the mind of every man, from the first to the lowest, the importance of the cause, and what it is they are contending for."[26] Washington would try hard to avoid irritating civilians by engaging in or tolerating behavior reflecting military arrogance. The General often bemoaned the plundering of civilian property and did what he could to prevent and stop that age-old practice. He even permitted his officers to mete out on-the-spot punishment of 100 to 150 lashes to soldiers caught plundering civilians.

Typically, in a General Order he denounced plundering American citizens as "highly disgraceful and unworthy of the Cause in which we are engaged. Add to this that it has a fatal & obvious tendency to prejudice their minds and to disaffect 'em."[27] Of course, troops were too scattered and command too decentralized to expect strict adherence to this and other of his orders, but he constantly pursued that worthy goal.

Additionally, the General carried out a humane policy regarding British prisoners and Tory opponents. While despising the Loyalists, Washington in a letter mused, "would it not be a good policy to grant a general amnesty and conquer these people by a generous forgiveness?"[28] His aide Tench Tilghman noted that the General "is blessed wherever he goes for Tory is protected in person and property equally to the Whig. And, indeed, I often think more, for it is his maxim to convert by good usage not severity."[29] Washington's leniency toward Tories led a critic to write, Washington "is so humane and delicate that I fear the common cause will suffer."[30]

Leniency was a wise and shrewd approach and was calculated, among other aims, to maximize the contrast between the British and American war efforts. Historian Robert O'Connell deals with this topic in his worthwhile book *Revolutionary*, arguing that the constant British atrocities played a key role in continually stoking the revolutionary fires.[31] The unending pattern of imperial atrocity operated like sequential jolts of electricity, recharging the Revolution's fervor and reinforcing the Patriot narrative. As a Patriot leader wrote, "The rapacity of the enemy was boundless, their rapine indiscriminate, and their barbarity unparallel."[32] O'Connell notes the surprising fact that German prisoners of war in Russia during World War II had a higher survival rate than American soldiers on fetid British prison ships during the American Revolution.[33]

Always better behaved than the enemy, His Excellency was instinctively magnanimous and more humane than his adversaries.

He was a revolutionary, make no mistake. But he was a conservative revolutionary who sought to diminish the war's terrible revolutionary potential.[34] His great contribution was to set a tone of moderation that kept his officers and men in check and the Revolution under control. He understood that this sort of war had an almost limitless potential for violence. If truly unleashed, the Revolution stood to consume itself in an orgy of retribution. Through sheer force of personality and an iron sense of decency, Washington functioned as the chief brake on the revolutionary excesses and worked to minimize retaliation against the Loyalists beyond the confiscation of their land.

Another of His Excellency's gifts to his country was that he recognized America's fundamental constitutional principle—civilian control of the military—even before there was a constitution. The commander in chief went to great lengths to prove his republican reliability by deferring to civil authorities on many matters when the ambiguity of the particular instance might well have justified his seizing the moment and taking independent action. This deference to civilian control was one aspect of Washington's leadership that his contemporaries found most heroic. And he kept this deference despite how often he was disappointed, if not outraged, by some of the actions of the Continental Congress: "It was one measure of his extraordinary self-control that this combative, fearless man allowed himself to be governed by prudence and his devotion to the republican ideal of the military to civilian authority."[35]

His reputation as a republican general was most cemented by his conduct during periods of what has been called his "dictatorship." When forced to flee Philadelphia, Congress granted him extraordinarily broad emergency powers to "direct all things relative . . . to the operations of war."[36] Washington's subsequent caution in exercising, or in choosing not to exercise, those emergency powers stamped him as a leader with more than a token commitment to republicanism. A French general marveled in 1782: "This is the 7th year that he has commanded the army, and that he has obeyed Congress; more need not be said."[37]

The best example of Washington upholding the principle of civilian control of the military was his handling of a crisis in the spring of 1783. Known as the Newburgh Conspiracy, the episode also reveals Washington's mastery of gesture as a tool of effective leadership.[38] While the details remain controversial, most scholars agree that the scheme, which had over- and undertones of a military coup, probably originated in Philadelphia, led by men like Robert Morris and Alexander Hamilton, who hoped to use the discontent among the army officers to prod Congress to pass a revenue bill and expand congressional power.

Certainly, there was a strong sentiment among many officers, perhaps orchestrated by General Horatio Gates, on behalf of the army refusing to disband until they were properly compensated for the sacrifices made to win the war. There was even talk of marching on Congress to reinforce those demands. General Washington, while sympathetic to valid complaints regarding compensation, heard talk of a meeting on that topic being planned. He rescheduled the conclave to meet on March 15, and then, unannounced, attended the meeting. Addressing his officers, he delivered one of his most impressive speeches, incidentally one that he wrote entirely by himself. He urged his officers not to threaten Congress, explaining that doing so would betray and besmirch their own ideals and service of the past eight years and would dishonor themselves and him. The idea that they might take up arms against their own country "has something so shocking in it that humanity revolts at the idea. My God! What can this writer have in view by recommending such measures?" he asked the assembled officers.[39] "Express your utmost horror and detestation of the man, who wishes, under any specious pretenses, to overturn the liberties of his country, and who wickedly attempts to open the flood gates of civil discord and deluge our rising empire in blood."

Having trouble reading a letter from a congressman supporting the officers, Washington, in a public first, donned his eyeglasses and solemnly declared to his frustrated subordinates, "Gentlemen, you will permit me to put on my spectacles, for I have not only grown gray but almost blind in the service of my country."[40] The resonant gesture of dropping his mask of command and revealing the man beneath brought tears to eyes around the room as men recalled his legendary sacrifices. The commander's display of human frailty in revealing that he needed glasses, an officer said later, was "superior to the most studied oratory." "It forced its way into the heart." With the skill of a dramatic actor, Washington demonstrated that eloquence did not require oratory. His accomplishment in defusing the Newburgh Conspiracy should not be underestimated. He stood before hostile men and changed their minds.[41] Washington won a battle at Newburgh as important as those he won at Trenton and Princeton and Yorktown, but this one was with his own troops.

That the army, disillusioned though its officers might be, was still even in existence in 1783 was remarkable. It had nearly been destroyed several times—but British mistakes, Washington's gift for improvisation and deft escape, and great good luck or providential intervention, depending on one's personal view, preserved the Continental Army.

Such might not have been the case but for Trenton and Princeton. No revolutionary events better illustrate Washington's perseverance, courage, aggressive strategic thinking, and decisive leadership than the three weeks culminating in the Battles of Trenton and Princeton at the end of 1776 and early 1777.

Thomas Paine, author of the famous pamphlet *Common Sense*, was in camp with the troops.[42] During that interlude, Paine penned a new work, *The Crisis*, which began, "These are the times that try men's souls." And so they were. Chased across New Jersey, Washington's army reached the comparative safety of Pennsylvania, but at the price of shedding stragglers as a wounded animal drips blood.[43] Washington confided to his brother Samuel, "Between you and me, I think our Affairs are in a very bad situation; not so much from the apprehension of Genl. Howe's Army, as from the defection of New York, Jerseys, and Pennsylvania. In short, the Conduct of the Jerseys has

Washington at the Battle of Princeton, published by Chappel, Johnson, Fry & Co., 1857. (Mount Vernon Ladies' Association)

been most Infamous. Instead of turning out to defend their Country and affording aid to our Army, they are making their submissions as fast as they can."

He concluded, "I think the game is pretty near up."[44] Nevertheless, Washington would not throw in the towel. As he wrote to Robert Morris: "I agree with you, that it is in vain to ruminate upon, or even reflect upon the Authors or Causes of our present Misfortunes; we should rather exert ourselves, and look forward with Hopes, that some lucky Chance may yet turn up in our Favor."[45] He declared, "desperate diseases require desperate remedies."[46] Or again, "Under the smiles of Providence, we may yet effect an important stroke."[47]

Indeed, General Washington did "effect an important stroke." The crossing of the Delaware River on December 25, 1776, is among American history's most iconic moments. Emanuel Leutze's famous painting may be wrong in many details—no such boats were used that night; Washington would have been a fool to stand at the bow of a small craft thrashing across an ice-filled river; and Leutze has the boat going in the wrong direction.[48] Even so, the painting brilliantly catches the spirit of the event and encapsulates Washington's charismatic leadership. As one soldier put it, "His appearance alone gave confidence to the timid and imposed respect on the bold."[49] Interestingly, the operation's secret password, which His Excellency composed himself, was "Victory or death." The decision was that risky.

Against all odds, the surprise attack worked. The Hessians were neither drunk on holiday cheer as legend has it, nor were they without advance warning. "Let them come," Colonel Johann Rall had declared earlier. "We will go at them with the bayonet."[50] Come the Americans did with devastating results for Rall and his command. Rall was mortally wounded and about nine hundred Hessians captured. With knowledge of Hessian atrocities circulating among American troops, the stage was set for possible retaliation, but Washington prevented any wreaking of vengeance. He paid his respects to the dying Rall. He permitted the Hessians to keep their personal baggage, and they were eventually sent to the interior, where Washington ordered that they be treated "with favor and humanity."[51] He even invited a few Hessian officers to dinner before they departed.

Learning of Washington's attack, the British commanding general, Lord Charles Cornwallis, canceled his impending return to England and angrily raced from New York City. Bent on capturing Washington's army at Trenton, he only narrowly failed to do so. Washington and his troops, many of whom had reenlisted after he urged them to do so with the heartfelt plea, "Your country is at stake, your wives, your houses, and all that you hold dear,"[52] managed once again to slip away. His Excellency ordered the army north toward Princeton. That risky decision put him in peril of being sandwiched between two British forces, but he felt the march was worth the gamble. In his words, "One thing I was sure of [is] that it would avoid the appearance of retreat."[53]

The mental image of General Washington's rallying his troops to victory at Princeton on January 3, 1777, is another one of the war's storied moments. At one point he was as close to enemy fire as a baseball batter is to a pitcher on a baseball diamond. A Philadelphia officer wrote, "I saw him brave all the dangers of the field, and his important life hanging as it were by a single hair with a thousand deaths flying around him."[54] Somehow, when the smoke lifted, the General, uninjured, was still astride his horse and calling out, "It is a fine fox hunt my boys," as the British retreated.[55]

These two daring and aggressive attacks, besides sapping British confidence, exerted an incalculable and uplifting effect on the colonists' morale. News of Trenton and Princeton swept across America like a rainstorm across a parched land, lifting bowed heads everywhere. And the raids were effective well beyond simply raising morale. Fearing more such incursions by Washington's army, now quartered for the winter at Morristown in northern New Jersey, General William Howe practically emptied New Jersey of British troops. Lightning raids, or the threat thereof, kept the enemy from setting up and protecting Tory enclaves with anything short of major power.

The Patriots had refused to collapse. In purely military terms, the New Jersey campaign was the most decisive of the war, at least prior to Yorktown. Indeed, Cornwallis himself declared after Yorktown, "When the illustrious part that your Excellency has borne in this long and arduous contest becomes a matter of history, fame will gather your brightest laurels rather from the banks of the Delaware, than from those of the Chesapeake."[56] Frederick the Great later wrote, "The achievements of Washington and his little band of compatriots between the space of ten days, were the most brilliant of any recorded in the annals of military achievement."[57]

When noted military historian Rick Atkinson summarized George Washington's first eighteen months in command, he could have appropriately been referring to the entire war. The conflict, Atkinson wrote, "had brought bitter lessons: that war was rarely linear, preferring a path of fits and starts, ups and downs, triumphs and cataclysms, that only battle could reveal those with the necessary dark heart for killing, years of killing, that only those with the requisite stamina, aptitude and luck would be able to see it through; and finally—the hardest of war's hard truths—that for a new nation to live, young men must die, often alone, usually in pain, and sometimes to no obvious purpose. Washington, more than anyone, would be responsible for ordering those men to their deaths."[58] In his own words, "Good God, what brave fellows I must this day lose!"[59]

George Washington had the requisite stamina, aptitude, and luck to see the job through to the end. Finally, at Yorktown in October 1781, all the pieces fell into place. Thanks to indispensable help from French naval forces and troops, Washington was able to trap Lord Cornwallis and his seven-thousand-man army on the Yorktown peninsula and force their surrender.

Contrary to folklore, British bandsmen did not play the tune "The World Turned Upside Down" as the troops marched out to lay down their arms, but they should have, for the world truly was being turned upside down. The official peace treaty in Paris would not be signed for nearly two more years, but in retrospect, Yorktown was clearly the decisive battle of the war which led to American independence.

General Washington's greatness as a military leader rests neither on strategic nor on tactical brilliance. After all, he lost considerably more battles than he won. His principal achievement was logistical—feeding, clothing, housing, equipping, and maintaining an army, never mind having created and trained that force, under dire conditions. His decision to inoculate his soldiers against smallpox was crucial in this respect.[60] Equally important, he regularly put aside personal grievances and insults in order to promote his larger goals and eloquently urged others to do likewise. In his words, "How strange it is that Men, engaged in the same Important Service, should be eternally bickering, instead of giving mutual aid!" he wrote.[61] "Officers cannot act upon proper principles, who suffer trifles to interpose to create distrust and jealousy. All our actions should be regulated by one uniform Plan, and that Plan should have one object only in view, to wit, the good of the Service." By keeping his army, the soul of the Revolution, intact and in the field, he wore down a superior opponent's resolve. That he was able to do so in the face of so many obstacles is a testimony to his greatness.

Learning of the official signing of the Treaty of Paris in the fall of 1783, Washington wrote a final Circular Letter to the states proffering wise advice for the newly independent nation and then prepared to end his military career. He bade a tearful farewell to his officers at Fraunces Tavern in New York City on December 4, 1783. One participant wrote later, "Tears of deep sensibility filled every eye—and the heart seemed so full that it was ready to burst. . . . The simple thought that we were about to part from the man who had conducted us through a long and bloody war, and under whose conduct the glory and independence of our country had been achieved, and that we should see his face no more in this world, seemed to me utterly insupportable."[62]

His Excellency had one more duty to perform to complete this chapter of his life, namely to return his military commission to a grateful Congress. To do so, he set out for Annapolis, Maryland.

5
RETURNING TO THE FRAY
1783–1789

THE FIFTH CHAPTER OF George Washington's life began on December 23, 1783. The moment was one for the ages. With perfect theatrical timing—one of Washington's many underappreciated talents—the General stood on the floor of the State House in Annapolis, the new republic's temporary capital, and formally returned to a grateful Congress his commission as commander in chief of the victorious Continental Army. The event was emotionally charged, and when the general spoke of his official family, he had to hold the manuscript of his speech with both hands.[1]

This voluntary surrender of great power struck observers as the last scene of a great historical drama: "So august was the spectacle! So moving were the acts! To see the beloved and unconquerable Hero surrender the insignia of his trust in subordination to the civil power . . . was an instance of moderation and greatness, noble as rare."[2] King George III apparently declared that if Washington actually did hand back his commission and return to private life, he would be the greatest man of his age.[3] The General did exactly those things in a gesture that was perhaps, as Joseph Ellis put it, the greatest exit in American history.[4]

With his improbable victory over Great Britain, George Washington had achieved that which, on a personal level, he most desired. He had won history's most elusive prize, fame across the ages—or what might properly be called secular immortality. Indeed, that prize was now his in a way that must have exceeded even his fondest expectations. Washington emerged from the war as his country's unrivaled hero and savior, far and away America's most beloved and admired figure, and famous throughout the Western world.

Rather typically, a French chaplain wrote, "Throughout all [this country] he appears like a benevolent God; old men, women, children all flock eagerly to catch a glimpse of him; people follow him through the towns with torches."[5] The president of Yale declared, "Oh, Washington, how I do love thy name! How I have often adored and blessed thy God for creating and forming thee, the great ornament of humankind!"[6] The poet Francis Hopkins declared Washington to be "the best and greatest man the world ever knew," adding that "had he lived in the [age] of idolatry, he had been worshipped as a god." And so it went. No American before or since has been so revered.

George Washington well understood that to enjoy the purity of a perfect heroism, a seeker had to be willing to attain that reward only in fame, not in material riches. His embrace of that equation and return to Mount Vernon and private life was so special as to generate comment across the Western world. Washington was not naïve.[7] He knew the effect his resignation would have. He was trying to live up to the age's fondness for the classical disinterested patriot, a man in the mold of Cincinnatus, who devotes his life to saving his country and then retires to his farm. But Washington's emulation of Cincinnatus was not merely a pose. It accurately reflected what Washington desired after a long, grueling, and ultimately successful war.

Arriving at Mount Vernon on Christmas Eve to be greeted by his dearly beloved wife, Martha, the General, now past the half-century mark in age, may well have believed that his life on the public stage was over. He was completely drained by over eight years of exhausting

The Resignation of General Washington, December 23, 1783, John Trumbull, 1824–28. (Yale University Art Gallery; Trumbull Collection)

service in behalf of his country. He knew he was from a family whose men died young. He had achieved all of his most important personal goals. What more could anyone ask of him? What more could he wish for? In a letter to his dear friend, the Marquis de Lafayette, he wrote, "I am not only retired from all public employments, but I am retiring within myself; and shall be able to view the solitary walk, and tread the paths of private life with heartfelt satisfaction. Envious of none, I am determined to be pleased with all; and this my dear friend, being the order for my march, I will move gently down the stream of life, until I sleep with my Fathers."[8]

But even while beset by depletion and exhaustion, Washington still pursued his "posterity project." Numerous portrait artists came to Mount Vernon, and he apparently sat for all of them; he encouraged his adoring aide David Humphreys to write a history of the war; and he welcomed to his riverside home the great French sculptor Jean-Antoine Houdon. Houdon stayed at Mount Vernon for over two weeks, following the General on his daily routine, and wrought what turned out to be the most lifelike rendering of the General. When Lafayette saw the bust many years later, he exclaimed, "That is the man himself." Houdon sought to portray Washington locked in unending struggle with his passions. Washington's raised right eyebrow, flared nostrils, and unsmiling lips all lead the viewer to see that here is a man of substance quietly fuming in indignation. But because he has his temper on a leash, the bust's distinctive gaze is undistorted by anger. (These points might be confirmed by carefully examining the portrait of the bust, which is the frontispiece of this book.)

As Washington explained to Lafayette, artists like Houdon were "the door keepers of the temple of fame" who held "the keys of the gate by which Patriots, Sages and Heroes are admitted to immortality."[9] Working with such artists was a price Washington was willing to pay. Few historical figures have so lovingly tended their image. Indeed, no one was better at self-promotion than Washington, but he did it in such a quiet, understated way that it did not seem to most people that he was doing it at all.[10]

His letter to Lafayette about quietly retiring at Mount Vernon contained an unacknowledged qualifier. What if he came to believe his country once again needed his service? Washington's love of country and his love of fame were intricately connected and cannot be separated. Much as he loved being the master of Mount Vernon, he loved his country and his fame even more.

In his 1783 letter to the states—his first farewell address—Washington noted that if America, with all its natural blessings, did not succeed, its people would have no one but themselves to blame. In his parting toast to his officers that same year, he proclaimed "Competent powers to Congress for general purposes." The message essentially foreshadowed the rest of his political life. His experience as commander in chief had made him skeptical of the states' claims to virtually total control of their actions and cognizant of the need for a stronger central government. The General always feared that excessive localism would undercut the effort at nation building.

Washington's paradoxical, yet remarkably prescient, position was that the rights and liberties of the people of thirteen states could best be preserved within a strong national union.[11] The parochialism and spirit of liberty that many thought essential to the preservation of those freedoms constituted a lethal virus carried by the American body politic. That virus stood to destroy the American Union and eventually liberty itself.

The years following the end of the War of Independence caused Washington great concern. He feared that the nation he had done so much to bring into being would not survive as a viable republic. Whether the thirteen former colonies, now independent states, collectively and individually jealous of their rights and privileges, and fearful of any move to empower a central government, could remain one single country was very much an open question.

Under the Articles of Confederation, the nation's first try at writing a constitution, the national government's reach was severely limited since it was denied taxing power or an effective way to implement national decisions. The individual states often clashed with one another rather than cooperating. In some states, debtors gained control of the legislature, and creditors faced the problem of having to accept virtually worthless scrip as payment for legitimate loans. The dangers of an "excess of democracy" seemed as real to Washington as the danger of British tyranny had a decade earlier.

Foreign countries showed little respect. Great Britain kept troops on American territory despite the Treaty of Paris. Spain denied American commerce the use of the Mississippi River. Barbary pirates seized and held for ransom thousands of Americans, and the country was too poor to ransom them and militarily too weak to stop the atrocities. Washington's own 1784 trip to inspect his Western properties illuminated for him the tenuous nature of America's hold on lands west of the Appalachians, reinforcing his conviction that the Articles of Confederation had to be dramatically revised to give the central government effective control over interstate commerce, foreign affairs, national defense, and its own revenue.

In short, in the minds of a growing number of renowned men who "thought continentally," America had entered a critical period, and unless remedies were discovered and applied quickly, the great experiment in republican government would fail. George Washington was certainly among that group.

Only a month after retiring from the army he was already writing to his friend Benjamin Harrison, "The disinclination of the individual States to yield competent powers to Congress for the Foederal Government—their unreasonable jealousy of that body & of one another—& the disposition which seems to pervade each, of being all-wise & all-powerful within itself, will, if there is not a change in the system, be our downfall as a Nation. This is as clear to me as the A,B,C."[12]

His letters in 1785 and 1786 are full of pessimism and foreboding. The country was fast approaching "the brink of the precipice," "a sea of trouble," "some awful crisis," "anarchy and confusion," or another similarly gloomy metaphor. Washington feared that the nation's newly won freedom was being squandered and that the people's rights might be lost to an even worse tyranny erected "on the ruins of Liberty abused to licentiousness."[13]

Whether he wished it or not, George Washington still carried the weight of a country on his shoulders. Thus, instead of enjoying a quiet retirement, he found himself in energetic correspondence with friends and leaders around the country, arguing that only a stronger and more energetic central government could preserve the Union. "13 Sovereignties pulling against each other," he observed, "and all tugging at the federal head will soon bring ruin on the whole."[14] As he wrote to one correspondent, "From the high ground we stood upon, the plain path which invited our footsteps, to be so fallen! So lost! It is really mortifying."[15] "Notwithstanding the boasted virtue of America," he wrote, "we are far gone in everything ignoble & bad."[16] Virtue, he feared, "has, in a great degree, taken its departure from our Land."[17] A letter to John Jay is typical:

> Your sentiments, that our affairs are drawing rapidly to a crisis, accord with my own. What the event will be, is also beyond the reach of my foresight. We have errors to correct; we have probably had too good an opinion of human nature in forming our confederation. Experience has taught us, that men will not adopt and carry into execution measures the best calculated for their own good, without the intervention of a coercive power. I do not conceive we can exist long as a nation without having lodged somewhere a power, which will pervade the whole Union in as energetic a manner, as the authority of the State Governments extends over the several States.[18]

Washington knew that increasing numbers of people were willing to consider switching to another form of government, even to a monarchy, if change would ensure order and protection of property. As John Milton long ago warned, "Most people prefer bondage with ease rather than strenuous liberty."[19] Yet, in Washington's words, "What a triumph for the advocates of despotism to find that we are incapable of governing ourselves, and that systems founded on the basis of equal liberty are merely ideal and fallacious!"[20]

Of course, Washington was not alone in hoping "that wise measures may be taken in time" to avert a calamity. There was a growing faction, spearheaded by men like James Madison, Alexander Hamilton, and other kindred spirits, which was arguing for a national convention to propose ways to strengthen the Articles of Confederation and assign adequate power to the central government. Frightened by Shays's Rebellion, an uprising by angry farmers in western Massachusetts in 1786, there was enough impetus to convene delegates representing the states at the Pennsylvania State House, now called Independence Hall, in May 1787.

It was unclear how decisive the convention would be. Earlier calls for a meeting at Annapolis came to nought following an abortive conference held at Mount Vernon seeking to improve trade on the Potomac

River. Certainly, a crucial component in any calculation was whether George Washington would accept his appointment and attend as a delegate from Virginia.

Washington faced a very serious dilemma: to go or not to go. Initially, Washington leaned strongly against participating. As he wrote, "Having happily assisted in bringing the ship into port & having been fairly discharged, it is not my business to embark again on a sea of troubles."[21] He had made a very public display of completely retiring from public life—of being the American Cincinnatus. Indeed, he had just told the Society of the Cincinnati, of which he was president, that he could not attend that august body's meeting, which, coincidentally was occurring in Philadelphia at the exact same time as that of the proposed constitutional convention. Washington feared his presence in Philadelphia as a delegate to the national gathering would appear disrespectful to and be resented by the members of the society. He also feared offending everyday Americans by seeming to break his promise to retire from public life.

Probably even more important, Washington had real doubts as to whether the time was yet ripe for extensive change. Declaring that "Ignorance & design are difficult to combat,"[22] he wrote his dear friend Henry Knox, "It is among the evils, and perhaps not the smallest, of democratical governments, that the people must *feel,* before they will *see.*"[23] He made a similar point to John Jay: "My fear is that the people are not yet sufficiently misled to retract from error!"[24] Had the people "felt" enough? If a major effort were made prematurely and failed, there might not be another chance to right the listing ship of state. Washington knew that prestige is like money: You only have so much. Did he want to spend his hard-earned reputation on the convention if it were likely to be a bust?

Finally, an important part of Washington desperately wished to spend his remaining years—which he expected to be relatively few—at his beloved Mount Vernon. He had to be convinced, and in search of that persuasion he wrote to friends like Henry Knox seeking candid advice as he was being "delicately pressed by many to attend."[25]

James Madison, Gilbert Stuart, ca. 1821. (Courtesy of the National Gallery of Art, Washington; Ailsa Mellon Bruce Fund)

Knox, one of the few men whom Washington declared that he "loved," urged him to attend in a way he knew would appeal: "Were an energetic, and judicious system to be proposed with Your signature, it would be a circumstance highly honorable to your fame . . . and doubly entitle you to the glorious republican epithet—The Father of Your Country."[26] Shays's Rebellion, seen through the reporting of Henry Knox, shocked the General: "If three years ago, any person had told me that at this day, I should see such a formidable rebellion against the laws & constitutions of our own making as now appears I should have thought him a bedlamite—a fit subject for a mad house."[27]

Further, one must not underestimate the gentle but remarkably cogent reasoning of James Madison, who spent much time at Mount Vernon in the early months of 1785 and developed an extremely close relationship with Washington.[28] Madison did much to convince the General that the meeting in Philadelphia was the last, best hope to repair the American experiment before it collapsed. Basically, it was a gamble, but it was one that Washington decided he had to make.

While a part of him did not want to go—in the same way that a part of him had not wanted to be commander in chief—it is difficult to imagine him staying away. In essence, he was a casualty of his own greatness, which steered him along a path from which, in the final analysis, he could not deviate. A sense of civic duty and a powerful urge to "be in the room where it happens," to quote the hit musical *Hamilton*, always trumped the idea of retirement at Mount Vernon. Furthermore, his fame could hardly be expected to light the ages yet to come if the revolution he had guided ended in failure.[29] His reputation "rode the fortunes of the country he had forged."[30] He had led the movement to win independence. He would now lead the movement to secure that independence and create a nation.

George Washington's contributions to the writing of the Constitution are difficult to assess but are by no means negligible. He wanted the delegates to "probe the defects of the constitution to the bottom, and provide radical cures."[31] His call for "radical cures" encouraged James Madison in the writing of the Virginia plan that became the starting point for the Convention. As one Virginian depicted the gestating plan, nothing less than a revolution in government was brewing. The basic idea was to alter the present federal system by substituting a great National Council with full legislative powers upon all matters impacting the Union. This sentence effectively summarized the Virginia plan. People would replace states as the building blocks of a national republic, and Congress would no longer have to go hat in hand to the states for everything. Washington embodied American nationalism in the United States. By setting that tone, he had a powerful impact on the Convention's work.

Not surprisingly, he was unanimously elected to preside over the Convention—another recurrent theme throughout his adult life. His first act was to have Virginia's governor, Edmund Randolph, present the Virginia plan, allowing no interruption of the governor's "long and elaborate speech." Clearly Washington sided with Virginia and its plan.[32] In this deft display of influence, he had helped to hijack the Convention. Congress had endorsed this gathering as a meeting only for the purpose to draft amendments to the Articles of Confederation. Washington's home state of Virginia instead proposed using the conclave to completely scrap the existing governmental arrangement and forge a nation.

His direct contributions to the resulting document were minimal, but Washington infused those who wrote the Constitution with a desire to win his approval. He could influence by a wink or a nod. His very attendance and subsequent appointment as presiding officer muted any carping about the Convention's patriotic credentials and focused attention on the event's importance. Washington's mere presence automatically made the gathering more significant than it could have possibly been had he not attended.

Washington presided with decorum and fairness over every single session during the four hot months from May to September 1787. As presiding officer, he was able to guide debate. He could choose which speaker to recognize, whether an angry voice or one inclined to conciliation. When someone violated the policy of secrecy and carelessly left a confidential paper vulnerable to discovery, Washington, after calling attention to the misstep, "bowed, picked up his hat and left the room 'with a dignity so severe that every person seemed alarmed.'"[33] The mere thought of a delegate admitting to the offense and being on the receiving end of his glare or worse prevented the anonymous miscreant from ever claiming the stray document.

As president of the Convention, Washington spoke rarely, but public oratory was not his strong suit. When he did step down and recommend that there should be one member in the House of Representatives for every thirty thousand people instead of the proposed forty thousand, his recommendation was unanimously approved. At countless dinners and meetings, Washington made crystal clear his endorsement of a stronger central government, and a reconstruction of the voting by the Virginia delegation confirms this. A great deal of what Washington wanted was in the final document.

He also influenced the finished product in an additional way. Establishing the presidency was the framers' most creative act, but that innovation left them profoundly uneasy because the notion of a vigorous executive was very hard to square with the prevailing bedrock republican ideas. There was no real precedent for the institution the framers conceived. The office of president, while hedged, as everything in the Constitution was hedged, delegated very significant powers to the holder of the office and made him independent of the judicial and legislative branches. He would serve for an unlimited number of four-year terms, appoint and supervise the heads of departments, serve as commander in chief of the armed forces, exert veto power, issue pardons, enjoy the right to call Congress into special session, and enjoy much latitude in leading the government in the conduct of its foreign relations.

The office of president was created specifically with George Washington in mind. According to one participant, the powers granted would not "have been so great had not many of the members cast their eyes toward General Washington as president; and shaped their ideas of the powers to be given to a president, by their opinions of his virtue."[34] With Washington literally before their eyes, the delegates were governed by their hopes rather than their fears. Interestingly, in ways often overlooked, Washington did a great deal to shape the presidency even before he occupied that office. At its core, this was Washington's Constitution, especially with respect to the presidency.

As presiding officer, His Excellency was the first to sign the historic document, and, in another act of tremendous faith in his integrity, the official journals of the Convention's proceedings were given to him for safekeeping.

Besides illustrating what the framers were doing and where, a work by Howard Chandler Christy illuminates in oil paint the themes of the proceedings. (The original is in the US Capitol and readily available online for readers who wish to view the portrait in color.) In Christy's painting, window shutters symbolically stand open with drapes pulled to reveal a bright new day. Sunshine backlights the figures, lending an almost religious aura. Obviously, Washington is the focal point of the painting. Sunlight streams into the chamber, highlighting him and simultaneously seeming to emanate from him as it reflects on

Signing of the Constitution, Howard Chandler Christy, 1940. (Architect of the Capitol)

Alexander Hamilton, Benjamin Franklin, and James Madison, who sit in front of the podium.

As members gather to sign the Constitution, some gesturing to be recognized, Washington strikes a statesmanlike pose. Compared to the other delegates, some of whom are wearing colorful and resplendent clothing, Washington is portrayed simply, yet elegantly, in a black suit. He is physically larger than anyone else in the room, particularly as compared to the delegate who is actually signing the Constitution. More importantly, Washington is not facing the Convention. Instead, he gazes into the future, undisturbed by the political jostling taking place before him. Christy's painting captures Washington as he sought to be remembered: standing above the political arena, not participating in the give-and-take of politics, instead influencing others by example and reputation.

Following the conclusion of their protracted and difficult proceedings, the delegates went to the City Tavern for a well-deserved farewell dinner hosted by Philadelphia's elite light-horse cavalry. It must have been some repast. The bar bill, which has survived, gives us a sense of the celebration:[35]

60 of Claret ditto.	21		
8 ditto of Old Stock	3	6	8
22 Bottles of Porter ditto	2	15	
8 of Cyder ditto	16		
12 ditto Beer	12		
7 Large Bowls of Punch	4	4	

The bill also specified compensation paid the musicians who performed at the dinner. Those bandsmen included:

	£	/	d
George Christhilf	1		
Mr. Schultz	1		
Mr Treniner	1		
John Keyser		15	
Wm. Hartung		15	
Philip Rotti		15	
David Kartzrock		15	
John Bruner		15	
Conrad Spangenberg		15	
	£7	10	

What a wonderful American story! The band almost certainly consisted of Hessians who originally had come to the New World as mercenary soldiers, hired to defeat the rebellion. They were captured, stayed in America, and now, as working musicians, helped celebrate the writing of the new Constitution for their adopted country.

Doubtless, George Washington's strong support for the new Constitution was absolutely essential to its being ratified by the required nine states. Although, because of a perceived conflict of interest, Washington refused to attend the Virginia ratifying convention in the summer of 1788, he lobbied hard behind the scenes for its ratification. "I never saw him so keen for anything in my Life as he is for the adoption of this new form of Government," one guest wrote about Washington late in 1787.[36] As he explained to a British friend, "A greater drama is now acting on this theatre than has heretofore been brought on the American stage."[37] To Washington, the real choice was to accept the Constitution drafted in Philadelphia or see the Union dissolve: "Thus believing, I had not, nor have I now any hesitation in deciding on which [way] to lean."[38]

He later declared the Constitution to be "the last great experiment, for promoting human happiness, by reasonable compact, in civil society."[39] Skeptics' attacks angered him. He became increasingly critical of those who opposed the Constitution and the methods they employed. That ire led him to break off his relationship with his former mentor George Mason over the way he believed Mason opposed the Constitution.[40] "Every art that could inflame the passions and touch the interests of men has been essayed," Washington complained.[41] "The ignorant have been told, that should the proposed Government obtain, their land would be taken from them and their property disposed of." Their forte, Washington said of the Anti-Federalists, "seems to lie in misrepresentation rather than to convince the understanding by some arguments."[42]

The importance Washington assigned to the ratification of the Constitution can be seen in a letter he wrote to Lafayette. If the Constitution is ratified, he asserted, "it will demonstrate as visibly the finger of Providence, as any possible event in the course of human affairs can ever designate it."[43]

Everyone recognized the importance of Washington's imprimatur on the new charter, which would reassure a public skittish about such momentous change. Nothing was more important to the Federalists' success than having Washington on their side. The critics' main claim was that the new government threatened individual liberty. The most effective response was that George Washington supported the new Constitution. "Is it possible that the deliverer of our country would have recommended an unsafe form of government?" a widely reprinted newspaper article asked.[44] Critics admitted as much.

An Anti-Federalist, Virginian William Grayson, who described Washington as "a host within himself,"[45] told one correspondent, "I think that were it not for one great character in America so many men would not be for this government." Following Virginia's ratification, James Monroe wrote Thomas Jefferson in France, "Be assured his [Washington's] influence carried this government."[46]

While he was pleased with the results—he called the document "an astonishing victory of enlightened reason over brutal force"[47]—the ratification of the new Constitution posed yet another dilemma for Washington. Would he accept the presidency? Virtually everyone except perhaps the man himself took it as given that he would lead the new government. Gouverneur Morris, penman of the final version of the Constitution and one of America's most perceptive, as well as one of its most sarcastic and wittiest, founding fathers, explained to America's hero why he must accept the office. "Your cool steady Temper is indispensably necessary to give a firm and manly Tone to the new Government," Morris told Washington, continuing: "No Constitution is the same on Paper and in life. The Exercise of Authority depends on personal Character; and the Whips and Reins by which an able Character governs unruly steeds will only hurl the unskillful Presumer with more speedy & headlong Violence to the Earth. The Horses once trained may be managed by a Woman or a Child; not so when they first feel the Bit. And indeed among these thirteen Horses now about to be coupled together there are some of every Race and Character. They will listen to your Voice, and submit to your Control; you therefore must I say Must mount this seat."[48]

Governor Edmund Randolph told Washington that many people supported the Constitution only because they were convinced that he would lead. Alexander Hamilton wrote his former commander and basically argued that by going to Philadelphia and helping to draft the new Constitution, Washington essentially became honor bound to accept the presidency and work to make the updated government a reality.[49]

Washington's reluctance to accede to these calls was genuine. The tasks facing the new president were daunting in the extreme. The aging Washington had no desire to face what he called "the 10,000 embarrassments, perplexities & trouble to which I must again be exposed in the evening of a life, already consumed in public cares."[50] After the war Washington had solemnly pledged to permanently retire, and at his advancing age he did not want to leave his much-loved Mount Vernon yet again: "The great Searcher of human hearts knows there is no wish in mine, beyond that of living and dying an honest man, on my own farm."[51]

Once again, George Washington was the victim of his own remarkable success. He desperately desired "secular immortality," fame across the ages, and, with his victory over Great Britain, he had achieved it. No American could ever hope to be more loved and idolized than he. Yet, as he considered the reality of becoming president, he had to face just how heavy a price that status carried. In historian Richard Norton Smith's analogy, unlike Faust, who was forced to pay the price of his ambitions by selling his soul, George Washington nevertheless discovered that the fame and veneration pursued over a lifetime could only be had at enormous cost.[52] He had achieved his goal by becoming the indispensable man, essential to the winning of American independence, but now his countrymen, with virtual unanimity, were calling for him to lead the new nation he had created. Nothing but death, illness, or disgrace could save the commander in chief from reemerging as president.[53]

Elias Boudinot, later secretary of the US Mint, understood Washington's dilemma but argued there was only one possible solution: "I feel your delicate situation—you have no choice in this great business—Providence and your Country call and there is no place for a refusal—the Sacrifice is required and the Offering must be made."[54]

Eventually, Washington came to agree with Boudinot. He feared "that my refusal might induce a belief that I preferred the conservation of my own reputation and private ease to the good of the country." In the final analysis, for Washington, the presidency was a "sacrifice of inclination to the opinion of duty."[55] "I fear I must bid adieu to happiness, for I see nothing but clouds and darkness before me."[56] Like the Roman patriot Cato, Washington's life was not his own when his country called.

Having reluctantly embraced his fate, he confided in a very rare introspective diary entry that he was preparing to leave Mount Vernon for his inauguration in New York City "with a mind oppressed with more anxious & painful sensations than I have words to express."[57] He came close in a letter to Henry Knox: "My movements to the chair of government will be accompanied by feelings not unlike those of a culprit, who is going to the place of his execution."[58]

In fact, the actual journey from Mount Vernon to New York was one long triumphal march, with rituals strikingly similar to those employed to welcome English monarchs on their "royal progresses" and their entries into London to be crowned. The president-elect's grand inaugural procession consummated America's love affair with George Washington. Floral arches welcomed him to Pennsylvania and New Jersey; mounted cavalry and light infantry met him in most towns; at every stop lavish banquets, clanging church bells, and booming cannons greeted him. To get a real-life glimpse of the father of their country appeared to be the fondest wish of every man, woman, and child. They demonstrated "the most undisguised attachment and unbounded zeal for their dear Chief."[59] Countless spectators later commented on how he seemed to catch their eye and bow to them. In Europe, people bowed to kings. On his journey to his inauguration, Washington continually bowed to the people as his way of acknowledging tributes and cheers. It endeared him to them, but he knew he was about to embark on a journey as challenging as when he accepted command of the Continental Army.

6

SECURING THE UNION

1789–1797

THE SIXTH CHAPTER IN the life of George Washington began on April 30, 1789, when he was sworn in as the first president of the United States in the national capital, New York City. The solemn inaugural ceremony took place at 26 Wall Street in Lower Manhattan on the second-story outside balcony of the recently built Federal Hall (replaced in 1842 by a new structure). Washington exactly repeated the constitutional oath—which did not include the declaration, "So Help Me God"[1]—accepting a new command that was to be approximately as long and as difficult as the roughly eight years he had endured as commander in chief of the Continental Army.

Washington had earlier written, "A great Mind knows how to make personal Sacrifices to secure an important general Good."[2] In this instance, the particular "important general Good" was the success of the American experiment in republicanism. If the only way to advance the cause was for him to sacrifice his personal peace and the joy of being under his own "vine and fig tree," then so be it. Interest, honor, and ultimately a desire for fame had led Washington toward supreme power and up a long and winding staircase at whose apex the air was thin and loneliness inescapable.[3]

If it was true that no president ever entered the office with more personal prestige and affection from the people than George Washington, only Abraham Lincoln and Franklin Roosevelt faced comparable crises, and one might argue that Washington's task was even more difficult. At first glance, the circumstances confronting Washington might not seem so extreme. Washington's "achievement must be recovered before it can be appreciated, which means that we must recognize that there was no such thing as a viable American nation when he took office as president."[4] Had Washington failed, there would have been no Union for Lincoln to save.

The constellation of tasks he faced was unbelievably difficult. Not only did he have to justify and flesh out the new office of the presidency, but he also had to knit together a new nation and convince a skeptical world that America's grand experiment in self-government was practicable. As Henry Knox observed, "Conduct and wisdom almost superior to the lot of humanity will be required in the first outset of the New Constitution."[5]

As with the Revolution, space constraints dictate an episodic accounting of George Washington's approach to the presidency, his philosophy, his main challenges, and the reasons for his success.

The determination to secure the Union defined his presidency, practically becoming an obsession. Without a strong Union, the former colonies would simply become "insignificant & wretched fragments of Empire."[6] He approached his tasks as president with the mindset of a strong nation builder. Washington was first and foremost a supreme nationalist. "George Washington, more than any member of the Revolutionary generation, both by word and deed, advanced the concept of an American nation," said historian Don Higginbotham, "and pressed for the creation of an institutional umbrella to bind Americans together."[7] Higginbotham suggested the perfect sobriquet for President Washington: The Unifier.

Washington's overarching goal was to strengthen the Union by avoiding the paralysis that had crippled the Confederation, at the same

George Washington's inauguration. (Mount Vernon Ladies' Association)

time proving that an effective government need not curtail liberty. The question for Washington as president was always what he could do—or avoid doing—to promote and strengthen the admittedly very fragile American Union: "Washington's ideas about constitutional power and nationalism were closely linked. He believed the revolution could only be secured if the states and their citizens gave their allegiance to a central government that was strong enough to protect the nation from external threats and internal threats."[8]

A window opens onto George Washington as president in a particularly interesting, forthright, and thoughtful letter he wrote to Catharine Macaulay Graham, a female admirer in Great Britain. Graham, a renowned historian, authored a much-lauded eight-volume history of her homeland. When she visited Mount Vernon in 1785 for what turned out to be a ten-day stay, Washington was clearly taken with her. Indeed, he was impressed enough that he noted in his diary, "I placed my military records in the hands of Mrs. Macaulay Graham for her perusal."[9] Washington genuinely liked and respected talented women and listened to them in a way most men of the eighteenth century did not.

The admiration was certainly mutual. Mrs. Graham could hardly contain her admiration for the General. "The more attentively Sir you are examined by the inquisitive mind," she wrote, "the more it finds, that the voice of fame, though noted for exaggerating the puny merit of mortals into a gigantic form of virtue, has in your case even lessened the truth."[10]

Receiving a flattering, congratulatory letter from Graham following his inauguration, he explained his expectations for life as president. He told her that only an "absolute conviction of duty" could have brought him back into public life again, writing, "The establishment of our new Government seemed to be *the last great experiment, for promoting human happiness, by reasonable compact, in civil Society.*" He continued, "It was to be, in the first instance, in a considerable degree, a government of accommodation as well as a government of Laws. Much was to be done by *prudence,* much by *conciliation,* much by *firmness.* Few, who are not philosophical Spectators, can realize the difficult and delicate part which a man in my situation had to act." (Washington's detractors might well be surprised that he used such language.) "In our progress towards political happiness my station is new; and, if I may use the expression, I walk on untrodden ground. There is scarcely any action, whose motives may not be subject to a double interpretation."[11]

John Adams, Gilbert Stuart, ca. 1800/1815. (Courtesy of the National Gallery of Art, Washington; gift of Mrs. Robert Homans)

He expected to undergo close scrutiny. "My political conduct must be exceedingly circumspect and proof against just criticism, for the eyes of Argus [the hundred-eyed guardian of the gods in Greek mythology] are upon me, and no slip will pass unnoticed . . . there is scarcely any part of my conduct which may not hereafter be drawn into precedent."[12] As he put it, "Many things which appear of little importance of themselves at the beginning may have great & durable consequences from their having been established at the commencement of a new general government."

George Washington as chief executive always strove to avoid unnecessary conflict and controversy. But he could not dodge the first snarl on his watch: what to call the holder of the job he now held. Vice President John Adams stirred that pot. Adams favored a ponderous title like "His Exalted High Mightiness" to reinforce the dignity of the office and to win respect from abroad. From a contemporary perspective, the issue might seem like an interesting but trivial sideshow, but at the time that topic agitated critics of the new Constitution. Many viewed Adams's penchant for fancy and verbose titles as validation of Patrick Henry's warning that the Constitution "squints toward monarchy."

Washington lamented that Adams had "stirred a question which has given rise to so much animadversion; and which I confess, has given me much uneasiness."[13] This episode soured Washington's view of Adams as a skilled politician and consensus builder and was a major reason why Adams remained outside Washington's inner circle even though their philosophies aligned and Adams was a man of vast knowledge and ability.

Fortunately for the new nation, George Washington was a master politician. Politics, at its core, is a layered form of performance art that he practiced so well that most people didn't realize he was a politician.[14] A French diplomat noted that the president demonstrated a "happy mixture of authority and modesty."[15] The British ambassador observed that Washington "possesses two of the great requisites of a statesmen, the faculty of concealing his own sentiments, and of discovering those of other men."[16]

The president would have agreed with Gouverneur Morris, who talked of "politics in the grand sense, or that sublime science which embraces for its object the happiness of mankind."[17] Being politically astute, Washington knew that perhaps his greatest single asset in his goal of strengthening the Union was the tremendous affection Americans had for him as the father of their new nation. In a real sense, he personified that nation. Before the country had symbols—a flag, a constitution, a national seal—there was Washington.[18] Today, the office of the presidency cloaks holders in prestige, but at the beginning, it was Washington's reputation that enhanced the office. It is difficult to imagine anyone else being granted trust and public confidence such that he could establish a stable and effective system of governance and convince most Americans that an energetic government was not incompatible with republican liberty.

An excellent example of how the first president used Americans' affection for him to strengthen the Union can be seen in his decision to personally visit every state. Historian Timothy Breen notes that the triumphal trip to New York to take office "brought home to Washington the possibility of an entirely new political theater in which he, as the lead player, would communicate to an adoring audience a powerful and compelling vision for the future of the new nation."[19] The numerous references to theater in Washington's correspondence strongly hint that he saw the world as a stage on which a person has a role to play. A lifelong lover of the theater and a devotee of classical drama, he grasped the essence of playacting, which he often employed, evincing a magnificent sense of stagecraft, whether to incite participants to action or bring them to tears.

It is not amiss to picture George Washington constantly "onstage" starring as a man indispensable to the successful birthing of a nation. He understood that he had it in his power to nourish the emotional bonds of patriotism that would help to render the fragile new federal system a reality in the lives of ordinary men and women. Washington's great presidential insight was to recognize himself as standing on a new national stage and to use that stage to bolster the nation's legitimacy, and he deserves high marks for taking the presidency to the people. As the initial "core of gravity," he bound the Union together as it worked through its first critical challenges. This alone was enough to make him the young republic's greatest asset and virtually its only adhesive.

Based on his experiences during the Revolution, Washington concluded that a strong national government was absolutely essential to establishing and maintaining an effective and genuine Union. Of course, his goal of establishing a strong central authority was elusive in a postcolonial environment fraught with deep public suspicion of any such entity. He had to contend with the fact that, at its very core, America's philosophy was steeped in distrust and fear of a consolidated central government. Patrick Henry and many others regarded any projection of executive power as a betrayal of the spirit of '76, a theme that still resonates in America nearly 250 years later, with a great many Americans viewing the government as a foe.

The issue of centralized governmental power came to the fore in the controversy surrounding proposals by Alexander Hamilton aimed at shoring up the nation's financial well-being. For the country to prosper and survive, the grave economic crisis facing the United States had to be at least eased and preferably resolved. The president gave his brilliant young secretary of the treasury virtually total responsibility to rescue the debt-burdened American economy. Hamilton's bold and dazzling plan, involving funding the debt, federal assumption of state debts, tariffs, and establishment of a national bank successfully resolved the immediate threat. Washington was soon boasting, "Our public credit stands on that ground which three years ago it would have been considered as a species of madness to have foretold."[20]

That success carried a grave price. A growing number of critics, led by Washington's brilliant secretary of state, Thomas Jefferson, and Hamilton's former collaborator, the equally gifted James Madison, believed that Hamilton's economic program benefited mainly speculators and the wealthy. Those players, concentrated in the Northern states, operated to the detriment of ordinary soldiers and farmers nationwide. In effect, Jefferson, Madison, and their allies believed the moneychangers had hijacked the temple, wresting the Revolution's original promise away from the people and into enemy hands. Hamilton's plan, they maintained, enhanced the power of the national government to a dangerous degree, threatening the rights of the states and endangering individual liberty such that the nation seemed to be on the verge of regressing into a monarchy.

The effort to block Hamilton's program set the stage for the development of political parties, although during Washington's presidency there were no parties in the modern sense of the term. Washington never accepted the idea of a "loyal opposition," viewing political parties as a dangerous threat to his vision of a united America. Washington's personal political philosophy left him ill-equipped to deal with the emergence of political parties. As a classical republican, Washington implicitly believed in a universal "public interest" to which virtuous men could unanimously subscribe.[21] Reality proved quite different. At the heart of the conflict between Hamilton and Jefferson was a clash of ideologies and wildly contrasting ideas of what constituted the "public interest." To Washington, the idea that there could be equally valid but contrasting concepts of the public good was utter nonsense, a heresy poisonous to good republican precepts. He never understood the value of the two-party system and the loyal opposition. Although he succeeded in developing national unity, he failed at promoting political unity. Many of his actions and decisions, perhaps inevitably, led to increased partisanship.

Warfare in the bosom of his official family drove Washington to despair. He worked feverishly, if unsuccessfully, to reconcile Alexander Hamilton and Thomas Jefferson. The president eloquently urged forbearance: "I would fain hope that liberal allowances will be made for the political opinions of one another; and instead of those wounding suspicions, and irritating charges, . . . there might be mutual forebearances and temporizing yieldings on all sides, without which I do not see how the reins of government are to be managed."[22]

As the break widened, the president commented on the tragedy of internal strife: "How unfortunate, and how much is it to be regretted then, that whilst we are encompassed on all sides with avowed enemies and insidious friends, that internal dissensions should be harrowing and tearing at our vitals."[23] Unless corrected, "in my opinion the fairest prospect of happiness and prosperity that ever was presented to man will be lost—perhaps forever!" To avoid unwanted controversy, Washington sidestepped fractious issues when possible. (For example, he did so on the issue of slavery.)

The president's first term was dominated by domestic issues—creation of the new government and the debate over Alexander Hamilton's plan to build a national economy, including his controversial federal tax on spirits, which triggered the Whiskey Rebellion. Seeing that conflict as a threat to the Union, Washington, conscious of both his reputation and the power of his image, donned his uniform and marshaled a massive thirteen-thousand-man force to crush the insurrectionists, although he only went part of the way himself.

As his initial term was growing short, President Washington, desperate to retire, had James Madison draw up a tentative farewell address. Washington had been gravely ill twice during his first term and was utterly exhausted—not only by the pressures of the office but also by the ubiquitous expectation that he be uninterruptedly wise and just. Even the most consummate performer tires of a role so demanding, a stance that sapped his every internal resource, day in and day out. He also feared that if he did not leave office, people would conclude "that having tasted the sweets of office, he could not do without them."[24] Washington's hoped-for retirement after his first term was not to be. While Hamilton and Jefferson agreed on almost nothing, they agreed that unless Washington served a second term, the young nation would fall apart. Jefferson expressed it well: "North and South will hang together, if they have you to hang on."[25]

Perhaps the most persuasive argument for a second term came from Washington's dear friend Elizabeth Powel, a truly remarkable woman and close confidante of the president. A fascinating letter from her to him demonstrates how well she understood the first president and how best to reach him. She saw the torment caused by a lifelong hankering after fame and the disillusionment bred by its consequences.[26] "Be assured that a great Deal of the well-earned Popularity that you are now in Possession of will be torn from you by the Envious and Malignant should you follow the bent of your Inclinations," Powel wrote. "They would say that you were actuated by Principles of self-Love alone—that you saw the Post was not tenable with any Prospect of adding to your Fame. . . . That Ambition had been the moving spring of all your Actions—that the Enthusiasm of your Country had gratified your darling Passion to the Extent of its Ability, and that, as they had nothing more to give, you would run no farther Risque for them."

Powel effectively painted a portrait of mean-spirited and envious men lurking in the shadows, poised to ravage his reputation and render his retirement torturously less serene than he envisioned. She continued, "For Gods sake do not yield that Empire to a Love of Ease, Retirement, rural Pursuits, or a false Diffidence of Abilities. . . . That you are not indifferent to the Plaudits of the World I must conclude when I believe that the love of honest Fame has and ever will be predominant in the best the noblest and most capable Natures. . . . And may you, till the extremest old age, enjoy the pure Felicity of having employed your whole Faculties for the Prosperity of the People for whose Happiness you are responsible, for to you their Happiness is intrusted."[27]

Washington reluctantly agreed to a second term and was unanimously reelected. He soon came to regret his decision. His near Olympian status in the life of the nation could not persist forever. America was becoming increasingly democratic, with a more bruising political style in the wings. The increasingly contentious political climate would make his second term a painful trial.[28]

Foreign affairs dominated Washington's second term, mainly in the form of the French Revolution and conflict over his support of the Jay Treaty with Great Britain. As for France, Washington's goals were national unity, social stability, sound money, and flourishing commerce. The French Revolution came to imperil all of these. France's revolution and its explosive rivalry with Great Britain "drew a red-hot plowshare" through the United States, with Jeffersonian Republicans favoring France and Hamiltonian Federalists backing England. As Hamilton's fiscal program did, the French Revolution engendered intense partisan divisions throughout the country and within the Washington administration.

The president found himself confronting perhaps the greatest test of his statesmanship. Grave foreign policy crises associated with the war in Europe collided with domestic crises arising from that war, dividing American attitudes toward the French Revolution. Washington survived by strapping himself to the Constitution while employing practical political guile acquired in the nearly four decades since he left the Virginia Regiment.

The crisis demonstrates George Washington's mature leadership better than any other case study. By 1793, France and England were at full-scale war, a conflict of such magnitude that it inevitably entangled the young and relatively weak United States, now deeply engaged in international commerce. Seeking additional American support, the controversial French ambassador Edmond-Charles Genêt, whom Washington came to despise, declared, "The cause of liberty is the cause of mankind, and neutrality is desertion."[29]

The president, a "rock-ribbed realist," disagreed.[30] He had summarized his philosophy regarding foreign affairs as early as the American Revolution: "No nation is to be trusted farther than it is bound by its interest, and no prudent statesman or politician will venture to depart from it."[31] He greatly feared that combination of excessive enthusiasm for the French, who publicly stood for "Liberty, Fraternity, and Equality," and the fact that until fairly recently, Great Britain had been fighting to keep its American colonies under the royal thumb could put the United States on a collision course with Brittania. Indeed, there was a growing movement in Congress, led by the Republicans, to impose economic sanctions on Great Britain in order to force the empire to better respect American neutrality. Great Britain was trampling American sovereignty, seizing not only American-flagged ships but also American seamen, as well as garrisoning and fortifying bastions within the territorial boundaries of the United States. In addition, Britain was aiding the Western indigenous tribes whose fight for autonomy on their historic lands was read by many contemporary Americans as bloodthirsty savagery for savagery's sake.

Washington's efforts to defuse the situation set the stage for the gravest crisis of his presidency and for what became both his most beleaguered but also his finest hour. To take Congress out of the equation, Washington appointed John Jay, then chief justice of the Supreme Court, as his special envoy. He sent Jay to England to negotiate a treaty avoiding war between the two nations. In so doing, Washington seized the initiative and assumed responsibility for resolving the crisis. This gesture defined the holder of the presidency as the nation's unrivaled leader in matters of foreign policy, a crucial precedent for America's future.

John Jay did obtain a treaty, but that diplomatic instrument disappointed Washington, obtaining as it did few concessions, chief among them a British vow to withdraw troops from American territory as promised earlier. The treaty basically accepted the British interpretation of neutral rights and granted Britain favored-nation status, eliminating future commercial discrimination against them for the ten years that the treaty was in effect. To the Republicans, led by Thomas Jefferson and James Madison, the Jay Treaty was a blatant sellout of American interests by an Anglophile—an example of toadying to Great Britain, a betrayal of France, and the reversion of America to neocolonial status, all but negating its independence. The bitterly anti-administration newspaper the *Aurora*, edited by Benjamin Bache, the grandson of Benjamin Franklin, predicted the

John Jay, from painting by Joseph Wright, *Century Magazine*, ca. 1888–89. (Library of Congress, LC-USZ62-95399)

treaty would lead to a complete political union of Great Britain and the United States, a prospect that "must fill the American mind with horror."[32] In Jefferson's harsh view, the Jay Treaty reflected treason rather than diplomacy.[33]

When the treaty's terms became public, widespread dissent and protest erupted. The president wrote, "The cry against the treaty is like that against a mad dog."[34] John Jay was burned in effigy along the entire Eastern seacoast. A newspaper editorialized, "Damn John Jay. Damn everyone who won't damn John Jay. Damn everyone who won't put lights in their window and stay up all night damning John Jay!"[35]

A crude poem portrayed Jay groveling before George III:

> May it please your highness, I John Jay
> Having traveled all this mighty way,
> To inquire if you, good Lord will please
> To suffer me while on my knees,
> To show all others I surpass,
> In love, by kissing of your—.[36]

Nevertheless, after much thought, Washington decided to sign the treaty, ratified by exactly the necessary two-thirds vote—20 to 10—in the Senate. While the story is very complicated, the basic reasons were simple. Despite its shortcomings, the treaty avoided war with Great Britain, provided a boon to domestic trade, promised essential revenue from tariffs, and bought the young nation time to grow and mature. Washington feared war would undermine his vision for a glorious American future and snuff out what he so eloquently had called "the sacred fire of liberty."[37] He was convinced that a period of peace was absolutely crucial to America's survival as an independent nation: "For sure I am, if this country is preserved in tranquility twenty years longer, it may bid defiance, in a just cause, to any power whatever, such, in that time, will be its population, wealth, and resources."[38]

His actions triggered howls of criticism, and no leader was more desirous of public approval and sensitive to criticism than George Washington. He suffered more direct criticism in his second term as president than during the rest of his life combined. And the presidency brought him none of the satisfaction of a victorious war.

The *American Mercury* asked, "Does the President fancy himself the grand Lama of this country, that we approach with superstitious reverence or religious regard?"[39] The *Aurora* urged the president to resign to "save the wreck of character now crumpling to pieces under the tempest of universal irritation." The editors derided him as a "supercilious tyrant," writing, "If ever a nation was debauched by a man, the American nation was debauched by Washington." James Monroe, who had been the nation's ambassador to France before being recalled, was so angry at the president that he declared that Washington had done more harm to the country in the last several years than any other individual.[40] Although he did not mail it, Monroe wrote the following: "The labours of yr more early life contributed to promote the liberties of yr country; but those of yr latter days to enthral & *enslave* it."[41] Such attacks had to have painfully stung a leader as desirous of public approval and sensitive to criticism as George Washington.

A good example of the shift in sentiment appears in the views of one of the most brilliant women of the revolutionary era, Mercy Otis Warren. Earlier, Warren had praised Washington as one "who has united all hearts in the field of Conquest, in the Lap of peace, and at the head of the Government of the United States." Now she wrote that the president was "much depreciated in my esteem." In a scathing criticism, she noted "his avarice of that base incense of adulation which he snuffs with avidity from every pen and every tongue of a servile generation."[42]

The president often professed indifference to such attacks, but in fact they tortured him. Jefferson wrote, "I think he feels these things more than any person I have ever met."[43] Jefferson recounted an episode in which Henry Knox showed Washington newspaper cartoons depicting him and John Jay being guillotined:

> The President was much inflamed; got into one of those passions in which he cannot command himself; ran on much on the personal abuse which had been bestowed on him; defied any man on earth to produce one single act of his since he had been in the government which was not done on the purest motives, said that he had never repented but once the having slipped the moment of resigning his office and that was every moment since; that by God he had rather be in his grave than in his present situation; that he had rather be on his farm than to be made emperor of the world; and yet they were charging him with wanting to be king.[44]

Washington's display was the honest outburst of a man feeling great frustration and anger after sacrificing so much for his beloved country.

Despite severe and, to George Washington's mind, unfair criticism, he was willing, in the manner of the high-minded Roman of classical lore, to promote what he firmly was convinced was the greater good of the country. In his words, "While I feel the most lively gratitude for the many instances of approbation from my country; I can no otherwise deserve it, than by obeying the dictates of my conscience."[45] Or again: "No fear of encountering difficulties and no dread of losing popularity shall ever deter me from pursuing what I perceive to be the true interests of my country."[46]

Most scholars agree that Washington's course was the correct one. That is almost always the case in studying Washington. One barrier to appreciating the depth of Washington's intellect is that what he said seems, in retrospect, to be obvious. But to identify, amid a complicated conflict, what the future would consider obvious, is a towering intellectual achievement. Washington's core quality was judgment, the capacity to make thoughtful and realistic assessments of the various options facing the infant American republic, and to make the correct decision every time.[47]

Finally, after eight long and difficult years in office, Washington voluntarily ceded power, maintaining that his deepest allegiance was thoroughly republican. His brilliant Farewell Address incorporates a thoughtful examination of the causes and dangers of unbridled partisanship, which the president prophetically called out as the greatest threat to American liberty.[48] He feared that "the spirit of party" would subvert the goal of unity that he worked so hard to build.[49]

Space prohibits cataloguing his many presidential accomplishments and precedents, led, perhaps, by the fact that Washington bequeathed to generations of successors a potentially powerful office, especially in the realm of foreign affairs. At the same time, he set high standards for the running of that office. He was a strong, energetic president but also one always aware of the limits on his office. He deferred to authority when appropriate but aggressively defended his prerogatives when necessary. In the words of one historian, "George Washington gave the United States something every nation needs, but few get: a national hero who understands that heroism includes giving up power and trusting your neighbor that integrity and virtue are a greater legacy than personal aggrandizement and national conquest."[50]

Washington's relinquishment of his office was the first of many peaceful transfers of power that would come to distinguish the American experiment. This phenomenon had no precedent. In a novel gesture with profound implications, the departing president again became an ordinary private citizen in all ways except those in which he was uniquely extraordinary. This was a fact of tremendous importance. As in his career as commander in chief, Washington's most important act as president was voluntarily giving up his office. He was the rarest of creatures, the indispensable figure who declared himself disposable.[51]

At the conclusion of the inaugural ceremony of John Adams, who had narrowly defeated Thomas Jefferson in the election of 1796,

Washington, always the master of the correct gesture, conspicuously emphasized the fact that he was now an ordinary citizen by pointedly insisting that Jefferson, the new vice president, precede him in exiting the building. He was enthusiastically looking forward to being just a private citizen again. Indeed, he compared himself to a child looking forward to a holiday.[52]

7
THE FINAL YEARS
1797–1799

GEORGE WASHINGTON BEGAN HIS life's final chapter on March 4, 1797, when John Adams succeeded him as president of the United States, and he again became a private citizen. Writing the day after his inauguration to his wife, Abigail, Adams noted that his predecessor's "countenance was . . . serene and unclouded. . . . Methought I heard him say, 'Ay! I am fairly out and you fairly in! See which of us will be the happiest!'"[1]

No doubt Washington felt relief at finally laying aside the heavy burdens of the presidency, and he was looking forward to returning to his beloved Mount Vernon, where he expected to live out his remaining years engaged in private endeavors. He said so explicitly in numerous letters, declaring he doubted he would ever again travel more than twenty miles from home, "Having taken my seat in the shade of my Vine & Fig tree."[2] (The arboreal image "vine and fig tree" was Washington's favorite phrase from the Bible, a source he quoted more than is generally recognized.) He would, he vowed, "spend the remainder of my days . . . in peaceful retirement, making political pursuits yield to the more rational amusement of cultivating the Earth." Quoting his favorite play, *Cato,* he declared he would view events in the "Calm lights of mild Philosophy,"[3] meaning that he would no longer be an active participant but only an outside observer.

Whether Washington remembered it or not, he had used almost the identical words following the end of the War of Independence in 1783, only to have circumstances repeatedly bring him back to center stage. Would that happen yet again? One might logically expect that George Washington, after close to a quarter century on center stage, was at last ready to enjoy a very well-earned retirement. Not so.

Washington's adult life reflected a constant tension between two conflicting impulses—his desire for autonomy and independence as the squire of Mount Vernon versus his desire to be shaping history at the center of power and influence. No matter how often he insisted that his only wish was to live and die an honest man on his own farm, his actions say otherwise. John Adams wisely noted, "He soon found Solitude, more fatiguing, more disgusting, and longed to return to public Bustle again."[4] Washington was not yet quite ready to watch the world pass him by without giving it a nudge or two.[5]

How did the ex-president once again end up on center stage? Several factors are worth noting. He had not retired with a sense of satisfaction. He was fearful about the future of the country and resentful of the attacks launched by his political opponents. From very early on in his supposed retirement, Washington subscribed to ten newspapers. He closely monitored what was going on with the new administration, at times taking the pulse of events more directly. On April 3, 1797, he wrote Secretary of the Treasury James McHenry, asking that he "communicate to me occasionally, such matters as are interesting."[6] McHenry and Secretary of State Timothy Pickering were only too happy to do so.

The most disturbing such news involved America's increasingly troubled relationship with France. The French viewed the Jay Treaty in 1795 and America's resulting accommodation with Great Britain as hostile and immediately began seizing American ships and confiscating their cargoes. French warships and French-commissioned

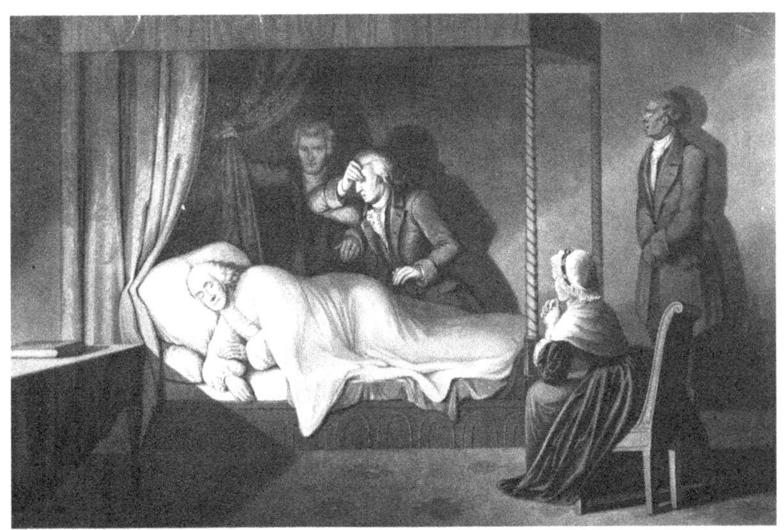

The Last Moments of Washington, engraved by Thomas Doney, after James Duthie, published by William Pate, 1861. (Mount Vernon Ladies' Association)

privateers had seized approximately three hundred American ships by the time of Adams's inauguration. France also warned that if taken prisoner by French forces, impressed American sailors serving on British ships would be treated as pirates. The situation as outlined by McHenry, Pickering, and others was grave. More worrisome, on the domestic front, the Republican Party of Thomas Jefferson and James Madison seemed happy to do France's bidding. Their actions led their opponents to label them "the French Party."

In response to events as he perceived them, George Washington, the man often viewed as being above party, became a highly partisan Federalist. The bitter opposition to the Jay Treaty, the extreme attacks on him by Benjamin Bache's *Aurora,* and Thomas Jefferson's devastating critique accusing Washington of having his republican principles shorn by the "harlot England" deeply distressed him.[7] When Washington's former ambassador to France, James Monroe, published a book savaging Washington's foreign policy, Washington responded in kind:

"The uncharacteristically angry, sarcastic, and acidly contemptuous tone of his comments rebutting Monroe's charges reveal how great a personal and emotional stake Washington had in the conduct of American foreign policy."[8] These and other attacks convinced Washington that his opponents were not merely wrongheaded but dangerous, even treasonous.

He declared the so-called French Party "the curse of this country" and a threat to American stability and independence.[9] Time would show the difference between those "who are true Americans" and "those who are stimulating a foreign nation to unfriendly acts, repugnant to our rights and dignity." The ex-president wrote, "A party exists in the U.S. . . . who oppose the government in all its measures. Those orchestrating this conspiracy are devoid of honor or any principle except the acquisition of power."[10] Washington told one correspondent that he was as sure that the Republicans had designs "of subverting their own government" as "that I am now in the act of writing you." They will "spread their poison in all directions."[11] So it had come to this: The judicious, nonpartisan, and moderate George Washington was now acting and talking like the most partisan, reactionary Federalists.[12] One cannot understand this aspect of Washington's career without bearing in mind that he harbored exaggerated fears of his opponents' motives and actions. He tended to confuse dissent with disloyalty.

The point of no return for George Washington was France's behavior during the XYZ Affair, so labeled because the French officials at the episode's core were not identified by name. Following his predecessor's example and hoping to peacefully iron out differences between the two nations, President Adams dispatched three American envoys—John Marshall, Charles C. Pinckney, and Elbridge Gerry—to France. The three endured numerous humiliations, foremost among them demands for a huge loan to France and personal bribes for the brilliant and wily French foreign minister, Talleyrand, before France would even begin negotiations.

When President Adams announced the failure of the mission in March 1798, the Republicans initially blamed Adams for making unreasonable demands. In April, however, President Adams released the commissioners' dispatches documenting how the French had threatened and attempted to extort the American envoys. Public reaction was stunning. The country raged at France. The catchphrase "millions for defense but not one cent for tribute" well expressed the depth of the national ire.

Washington learned the backstory of France's intransigence and hope of conquest from John Marshall, one of his favorite individuals. Marshall wrote Washington a long, detailed letter in early March 1798 outlining France's actions. Washington was shocked: "What a scene of corruption and profligacy have these communications disclosed."[13] Polish nobleman Julian Niemcewicz, who visited Mount Vernon on June 13, 1798, recorded in his journal that Washington had read aloud from Marshall's letter, then fulminated. "I never heard him speak with so much fire and candor," the Pole wrote. He quoted Washington as saying, "Whether we consider the wrongs and the plunder which our trade is suffering or the outrage to the independence and to the dignity of the nation in ejecting our ministers, or whether we think at last of the oppression, ruin, and destruction of free nations produced by this military government, we always see the necessity of Arming ourselves with a power and cunningness equaling the danger which threatens us. Patience and submission will not avail us anymore than it did Venice. Submission is cowardice. Rather than that, America will arouse; every one of us, myself in spite of my age, will give all the blood that remains in my veins."[14]

Events seemed bound to yank Washington from beneath the shelter of his proverbial vine and fig tree. In retrospect, the course of events conveys an air of inevitability. After all, who should command the new army and save the country from France? Who else but the man who had freed the young nation from Great Britain? President Adams recognized this from the first. "We must have your name, if you, in any case, will permit us to use it," he wrote to Washington. "There will be more efficacy in it, than in many an army."[15]

George Washington responded to the call with alacrity—more so than he had in 1775, certainly more so than he had in 1789. A sign of his willingness to serve may be seen in Washington's decision to write President Adams in early June 1798. In his first communiqué to his successor since the latter's inauguration, the former president praised Adams's tough stance against France and cordially invited him to Mount Vernon—a first.[16] Washington confessed to Secretary of War McHenry that he would find it difficult in a crisis like the one at hand "to remain an idle spectator under the plea of age or retirement."[17]

As always, there came disclaimers, and at one level they were no doubt heartfelt. Washington emphasized that he did not want to leave Mount Vernon and "the tranquil walks of retirement."[18] He told Alexander Hamilton that he would "go with as much reluctance from my present peaceful abode, as I should go to the tombs of my ancestors."[19] He worried that critics might view his taking command as "a restless act" or that the country might think that his professed love of retirement "was all a sham." He fretted about whether "my strength and powers might be found incompetent."[20] Was he too old? He noted that however desirous one might be, one could not simply strike forty years off one's age.

At the same time, he made clear to Hamilton and to the secretary of war that he would respond "if a crisis should arrive when a sense of duty, or a call from my country, should become so imperious as to leave me no choice."[21] Certain conditions had to be met. After all, Washington was once again risking his well-deserved reputation, and he needed to be in control of certain factors. Crucially, he had to be able to appoint the army's highest-ranking officers, especially the men of his general staff.

President Adams might well have inferred from Washington's letters and from discussions with cabinet members that he was going to agree to serve. For whatever reason, the president decided to act before receiving Washington's official agreement to accept the commission.

Adams nominated George Washington, and the Senate "unanimously confirmed" him to be "Lieutenant General and Commander-in-Chief of all the Armies raised or to be raised for the service of the United States." This was the fifth *unanimous* instance of the country calling Washington to an important post, proof of his unparalleled stature.

Adams's premature gesture led to three months of conflict and confusion entangling three very prominent Americans—Washington, Adams, and Hamilton—none of whom emerged from the squabble with an enhanced reputation. At heart, the dispute was actually quite simple. George Washington strongly desired Alexander Hamilton to be his second in command. John Adams absolutely did not want to appoint Hamilton to that very important position. The newly created army's first battle would be between two commanders in chief.

Washington fervently believed that he needed to have the power to control his choices of staff. In a sharply worded letter to Adams, he wrote, "It was the ground on which I accepted and retained the commission."[22] And he strongly insisted that Alexander Hamilton be inspector general and second in command, even though Hamilton had not held a high rank in the War of Independence. Senior officers' rankings held particular importance because of another of Washington's conditions. The General would assume functional command of the army only if France actually invaded the United States. Until that invasion occurred—a distant possibility—whoever was second in command would be the de facto commander.

By placing conditions on his acceptance and insisting on naming his general officers, Washington was setting the stage for trouble by tacitly undermining the president as commander in chief.[23] It was a serious mistake. Doubtless, Washington would have rejected such conditions were he president. Greatly compounding the situation was John Adams's profound distrust of and visceral dislike, if not outright hatred, for Alexander Hamilton. Among other imprecations, Adams had called Hamilton that "bastard brat of a Scottish peddler" and "the most reckless, impatient, artful, indefatigable, and unprincipled intriguer in the United States if not in the world."[24] Obviously, Adams didn't want such a man as de facto commander of the army.

Furthermore, as president, Adams clearly felt the choice of senior officers to be his prerogative. In frustration, Adams asserted that if he could make Washington president, he would do so, "but I never said I would hold the office & be responsible for its exercise, while he should execute it."[25] In the final analysis, the president had little choice but to accede to Washington's demands. The ex-president had all the leverage. As Adams later recalled, "I was no more at Liberty than a Man in a Prison, chained to the floor and bound hand and foot."[26]

In November 1798 Lieutenant General George Washington entered Philadelphia with full military flair, on horseback and in uniform, flanked by a troop of cavalry. Almost the entire military corps was drawn up on the commons to receive him. Did the event summon memories of his successful role as the commander in chief of the Continental Army? Washington left no comments, but there is no question that once again he wanted to look the part of a commanding general, as he recognized that part of successfully exercising command came from looking the part. He had asked his good friend William Fitzhugh to keep an eye out for a suitable "horse of figure," preferably a "perfect white."[27] Ordering a new uniform, he instructed his tailor, "Let your blue cloth be of the best & softest French or Spanish; and the finest you can procure, of a deep color. And the Buff of the very best sort."[28] That uniform was to be embroidered with gold thread, but his tailor, despite great effort, could not obtain any in time for Washington to wear his new uniform in active command or at his step-granddaughter Nelly's wedding on February 22, 1799. The uniform was never delivered.

The Quasi-War with France fizzled to a finish. President Adams may have lost control of the army, but he dominated the peacemaking. For domestic reasons, France signaled to Adams a willingness to negotiate an end to the conflict. In time, a treaty was signed, but word of that pact arrived too late to materially help Adams in his bitter 1800 presidential contest against Thomas Jefferson.[29]

Washington returned to Mount Vernon thoroughly disillusioned with the ways of American politics—though not to the point of disengaging from them. He was soon urging allies like Patrick Henry, a late convert to Federalism, and Light-Horse Harry Lee to run for seats in the Virginia state legislature, as he had earlier encouraged his nephew, Bushrod Washington, and John Marshall.

Would Washington himself consider running again for president in 1800 to save the country from a "French Party" president? His initial response was to say no way. In this new era of democratic party politics, Washington sadly concluded that "personal influence" and "distinctions of character" no longer mattered. If the members of the Jeffersonian Republican Party "set up a broomstick" as candidate and called it "a true son of Liberty" or "a Democrat" or "any other epithet that will suit their purpose," Washington argued, the stick would still "command their votes in toto."[30]

Could anything have changed his mind? We will never know because death intervened. John Adams later theorized that had Washington lived, he would have run—and he would have won.[31] Certainly, one could point to numerous instances in which Washington declared that he was finished with public service, only to be persuaded reluctantly or to vault eagerly back into the arena. Interestingly, as late as September 1799, he was making arrangements to manage Mount Vernon, "if I should not be called into public service of the country."[32]

Had he lived, run, and won rather than passing power on to less extraordinary men, his enduring status as "first in war, first in peace, and first in the hearts of his countrymen" would have been irreparably damaged. Much like Abraham Lincoln, George Washington, as far as his historical reputation was concerned, died at the optimum national moment.

Even heroes eventually grow old and die. During his presidency, George Washington survived two close encounters with death, one from a very large, seriously infected carbuncle on his thigh and the other from a bout with pneumonia. After his final retirement, he intuited that his remaining time on earth was likely to be very brief. He was acutely conscious that he came from "short-lived" stock, his father dying at the age of forty-nine, and his grandfather and elder siblings all succumbing even earlier in their lives. While not given to morbid thinking, Washington knew well the impartial cruelty of time passing. With surprising frequency in his correspondence, he remarked on his mortality.

He was not being theatrical but rather displaying a firm grasp on reality. He owned and had read the works of the Stoic philosopher Marcus Aurelius, who wrote, "It is the duty of a thinking man to be neither superficial, nor impatient, nor yet contemptuous in his attitude towards death, but to await it as one of the operations of Nature which he will have to undergo."[33] Death is a debt—a debt to nature—that everyone must pay.

For whatever combination of reasons, George Washington was not afraid of death. Thomas Jefferson wrote that Washington "was incapable of fear."[34] He reacted to his first battle by describing the whistle of enemy bullets passing nearby as "charming." His legendary courage as commander in chief of the Continental Army might have unnerved his aides, but it inspired his troops. In his view, a man's death was to be envied if it brought him honor and glory. Strengthening his ability to calmly face mortality was his conviction that he enjoyed providential protection. During one of his close brushes with death while president, he explained to Dr. Samuel Bard why he was the calmest person in the room: "I know that I am in the hands of a good Providence."[35]

While Washington certainly believed in an afterlife, he was ambivalent as to its nature and paid the topic surprisingly little attention. The available evidence suggests that he cared more about the immortality of his legacy than he did about the immortality of his soul. Certainly, he made an occasional positive reference to a happy future after death—"life in the hereafter" as he occasionally termed it. When his beloved Patsy, Martha's daughter from her first marriage, suddenly succumbed to an epileptic seizure at the age of only seventeen,

Washington wrote that "this sweet innocent girl entered into a more happy and peaceful abode than any she has met with in the afflicted path she hitherto has trod."[36]

More commonly, Washington painted the afterworld in grimmer shades. He wrote about his "approaching decay," the "house of my dissolution," of going "to the shades of darkness," "to sleep with my Fathers," to "the shades below," "to the tomb of my ancestors," "to the dreary mansions of my Fathers." Death was "that country from whence no Traveller returns."[37]

Perhaps the most striking aspect of Washington's view of life after death centers on what he did not say. Not once in all of his authenticated extant correspondence did he explicitly indicate any belief in the reunion of loved ones in heaven. Certainly, the greatest comfort of religion in general and of Christianity in particular is this hope. Washington may have urged grieving individuals to seek consolation in doctrine, but in his letters of condolence he never told addressees they would meet a departed loved one in heaven.

Neither did he comfort himself with such a vision. Indeed, to the degree that he wrote about death, he emphasized separation. After his favorite brother Jack's death, he lamented that he had "just bid an *eternal farewell* to a much-loved Brother."[38] After visiting his mother, who was dying of breast cancer, he confided to his sister, "I took a final leave of my Mother, *never* expecting to see her more."[39] After parting from his beloved friend, the Marquis de Lafayette, Washington pined, "I often asked myself, as our Carriages distended, whether that was the last sight, I ever should have of you? *And tho' I wished to say no—my fears answered yes.*"[40] These assertions and others were not tempered with qualifiers such as "in this world."

George Washington's life ended quickly and unexpectedly. Death was not likely to have been on his mind as he went out to check on his various farms on Thursday, December 12, 1799. Lately his health had been robust, and he was eagerly looking to the future. In the preceding weeks, for example, he had formulated a meticulous and remarkably detailed plan for managing his Mount Vernon farms, setting down precisely what was to be done over the next three years. This prospectus fills twenty-two pages in the printed edition of his papers.[41] George Washington was clearly not done living when he died.

He remained outside that Thursday for approximately five hours despite the fact that, as he described it, "the weather was very disagreeable, a constant fall of rain, snow and hail with a high wind."[42] Returning to the house wet and chilled, with snow still clinging to his hair and coat, Washington opted to dine without changing clothes.

The next afternoon, despite harsh, sleeting weather and that he was presenting symptoms of a cold and sore throat, Washington nonetheless briefly went outside in the afternoon to mark some trees he wanted felled. By that evening, he was very hoarse, albeit in good spirits. He insisted on reading sections of the newspaper aloud to his faithful personal secretary, Tobias Lear, making what turned out to be his final political comments. Tellingly, he expressed his annoyance at reports of actions by Thomas Jefferson's two top lieutenants, James Madison and James Monroe.[43] That evening he made what would be his final entry in his diary. Fittingly for a compulsive record keeper, his last written words, "Mer[cury] 28 at night," were a measurement.[44]

There is a wonderful snippet in the play *The Lion in Winter,* in which a character, referring to death, asks, "What does it matter how a man falls?" Washington would have seconded playwright James Goldman's response: "It matters a great deal when falling is the only thing left to do."[45] His death would be the last act of George Washington's remarkable life, and he wanted to exit the stage in the proper manner. When his sole surviving brother, Charles, died in September 1799, Washington wrote, "I was the first, and am now the last, of my fathers Children by the second marriage who remain. When I shall be called upon to follow them, is known only to the giver of life. When the summons comes, I shall endeavour to obey it with a good grace."[46] Having numerous times faced death so bravely and so calmly, he fully expected to meet the mortal summons "with a good grace." Little did he imagine just how difficult the final challenge would be. (Many accounts of his last hours describe Washington's death as peaceful. It was not.)

By the early hours of Saturday morning, December 14, his condition had deteriorated so rapidly that he awoke in considerable discomfort and with labored breathing. While certainty is not possible, the latest and most convincing medical studies indicate that George Washington died from acute epiglottitis caused by virulent bacteria.[47] The epiglottis is a flap of tissue that keeps the airway to the lungs clear of food and liquid when swallowing. An infected epiglottis can swell so much that it compromises breathing and renders swallowing a terrifying ordeal.

Now George Washington was fighting air hunger, gasping for each breath against his body's reflexive effort to smother him. Throughout the day he restlessly fidgeted, struggling and failing to find a position that would relieve his desperation. He was slowly suffocating, an agony heightened by the difficulty of trying to convey his wishes between gasps.

There was not one thing done for or to the failing Washington during those hours by his physician and close friend of over forty years, Dr. James Craik, and others that was not done in love and with the very best of intentions. Yet virtually all of his caregivers' actions compounded his suffering, and perhaps even hastened his demise.

Even simple ministrations conspired against their august patient. "A mixture of Molasses, Vinegar & butter was prepared to try its effects in the throat; but he could not swallow a drop," Lear recounted.[48] "Whenever he attempted it, he appeared to be distressed, convulsed and almost suffocated." In keeping with medical doctrine of the day, Washington was bled four times in sanguinary procedures that drained him of over eighty ounces of blood. His body was blistered painfully. Purgatives and emetics induced diarrhea and vomiting. The resulting discomfort these efforts would inflict on a patient struggling to swallow and gasping for every breath beggars calculation. The room must have reeked of "blood and stench and sweat."[49] Indeed, his final hours had to have been hellish.

The General's response to these torments is very revealing. George Washington "died as he lived," demonstrating courage, sense of duty, sensitivity, and modesty while conveying important instructions to those at hand. A matter very much on his mind was his final will and testament, a twenty-nine-page document that he had written out by hand the previous summer.[50] He now asked his dearly beloved wife, Martha, to retrieve that instrument and an earlier version, which he instructed her to burn.

Very significantly, in what was essentially George Washington's last act, he revised his will and set up a plan to provide freedom for all the enslaved workers to whom he held title; by law, he could not free those belonging to his wife and the Custis estate. A friend had earlier written Washington that freeing his enslaved workers would "give the finishing stroke and last polish to your political character."[51] Exactly. George Washington wanted very much to be on the right side of history.

With death imminent, Washington's other major concern was for his vast personal archive. It is not coincidental that the dying hero's longest speech, when speech was so very difficult, addressed the disposition of his personal papers. This intense focus reflected Washington's yearning for fame and secular immortality. He actually planned to build a structure to house his archives—in essence, a pioneering presidential library.

Grace amid danger figured prominently in Washington's code of honor, and the ultimate test of honor was courage in the face of one's own death. This was a rare strength, and he once again lived up to his creed. An old Spanish proverb declares, "It is one thing to talk about the bull in the ring. It is another thing to be in the ring with the bull." George Washington was able to face the bull in the ring.

In Joseph Ellis's succinct phrase, Washington "died like a Roman Stoic, not a Christian saint."[52] Certainly, he needed all of his resources to see his ordeal through to its end. He expressed both the difficulty of the journey and his confidence, telling Dr. Craik, "I die hard, but I am not afraid to go."[53] His dear friend Bryan Fairfax called that

that such of the latter description as have no parents living, or if living are unable, or unwilling to provide for them, shall be bound by the Court until they shall arrive at the age of twenty five years; — and in cases where no record can be produced, whereby their ages can be ascertained, the judgment of the Court upon its own view of the subject, shall be adequate and final. — The Negros thus bound, are (by their Masters or Mistresses) to be taught to read & write; and to be brought up to some useful occupation, agreeably to the Laws of the Commonwealth of Virginia, providing for the support of Orphan and other poor Children. — and I do hereby expressly forbid the Sale, or transportation out of the said Commonwealth, of any Slave I may die possessed of, under any pretence whatsoever. — And I do moreover most pointedly, and most solemnly enjoin it upon my Executors hereafter named, or the Survivors of them, to see that this clause respecting Slaves, and every part thereof be religiously fulfilled at the Epoch at which it is directed to take place; without evasion, neglect or delay, after the Crops which may then be on the ground are harvested, particularly as it respects

Go: Washington

Page from George Washington's will, which outline his plans for manumission for enslaved workers. (Fairfax County Circuit Court Historic Records Center)

statement "a great thing from him, because he was one of the last Men to complain. One Expression of that sort from him, to me shews more Suffering than 100 Groans from almost any other Man."[54]

As the microbial storm ravaged his body, it became increasingly clear that this was a tempest that even the heroic George Washington could not weather, although his robust physique probably prolonged his dying. Knowing the end to be near, Washington, always desirous of being in control, feared being mistaken for dead and buried alive, a more realistic concern then than now. For whatever reason, the issue was obviously of the utmost importance to him. After several unsuccessful efforts, he at last managed to convey his final request to the faithful Lear. He was not to be buried for at least two days after being pronounced dead.[55] When Lear, choked up with emotion, simply nodded, Washington pressed him, "Do you understand me?" Lear said that he did, whereupon Washington uttered his last recorded words, "tis well."

Ever shorter on oxygen and ever more burdened by carbon dioxide, the General's lungs shut down. Dr. Craik was lost in the grief of being unable to save the man he so loved. As Washington lapsed into unconsciousness, he closed his eyes. He had been taking his own pulse. That hand fell to his side, his countenance changed, and he then "expired without a struggle or a sigh."[56] "The great body, which had endured so much, the great mind, so steady in its operation, so sure in its conclusions, was all stilled. Here was no more than an empty vessel, drained for the subsistence of a nation."[57]

George Washington died as he lived, meeting his final test on earth with such grace and courage and character as to affirm the dignity of man and command respect and admiration. Thomas Jefferson aptly quoted the Bible on David's response to Saul's death: "Verily a great man hath fallen this day in Israel."[58] So he had.

In the context of actual events, Washington's final utterance, "tis well," is mundane. In a broader sense, though, his words are perfectly apt. Facing death, George Washington could review his extraordinary life as a whole and conclude, "Tis well." What a remarkable man he was, and what a gift he gave to mankind and to his beloved country. Among the founding fathers of the “great unfinished symphony” that is America, George Washington holds a place unique and immortal—first and always. Without him, the great experiment in republican government never would have had the chance to thrive.

AFTERWORD

George Washington and Slavery

> The grating chain of racism and slavery snaked through the new republic and diminished every life it touched.
>
> —ROGER WILKINS, *Jefferson's Pillow: The Founding Fathers and the Dilemma of Black Patriotism*

THE VEXING QUESTION OF how to deal with the issue of slavery, both in his own life and in the life of the nation he founded, bedeviled George Washington for the last twenty-plus years of his life. He referred to slavery as "the only unavoidable subject of regret."[1] In frustration, he confessed to a friend, "I shall frankly declare . . . that I do not like even to think, much less talk of it."[2] While his admirers might in similar fashion want to wish away the reality of slavery, the topic's importance demands that it be addressed and that George Washington's role in it be examined.

The twenty-first century is a particularly difficult American era for the reputation of any founding father who held people in bondage, regardless of how significant his contributions may have been. Indeed, many commentators seem to revel in a certain "ecstasy of sanctimony,"[3] calling out the moral failing and hypocrisy of men who declared all men were created equal and entitled to liberty, while at the same time they enslaved fellow human beings. When a group of schoolchildren were asked recently to give one fact about George Washington, the majority answered that he was a slaveholder. He owned other human beings! After touching on Washington as a slaveholder, the author of a prize-winning book on George Washington declared that we must all agree that the real George Washington is "not one of us."[4]

Prior to the War of Independence, George Washington's attitude toward slavery was as callous as that of a typical Virginia planter: "Sir: With this letter comes a Negro (Tom) which I beg the favor of you to sell, in any of the Islands you may go to, for whatever he will fetch, & bring me in return for him: one hhd of best molasses, one ditto of best Rum, one barrel of Lymes—if good and Cheap, . . . And the residue, much or little, in good ole Spirits. That this Fellow is both a Rogue and a Runaway . . . I shall not pretend to deny—But . . . he is exceeding healthy, strong, and good at the Hoe . . . which gives me reason to hope he may, with your good management, sell well (if kept clean and trimmed up a little when offered for sale . . . [I] must beg the favor of you least he shoud attempt his escape) to keep him handcuffed till you get to Sea."[5]

In 1769, while urging the sale of slaves belonging to his debt-ridden neighbor John Posey, Washington noted, "It is a fact well known that his Negroes & stock never can be disposed of at a more favorable juncture than in the Fall when they are fat and lusty."[6] On the eve of the Revolutionary War, Washington showed neither an inclination to reduce his investment in enslaved workers nor any reluctance to participate in public slave sales, such as the widely advertised George Mercer auction that Washington managed in 1774. As virtually any aspiring Virginia planter would have done in the middle of the eighteenth century, George Washington built up his enslaved labor force to increase both his wealth and prestige.

Seen in historical perspective, could one realistically expect any other behavior? Given his boyhood, how could young Washington have matured into anything other than a man who simply accepted slavery as a fact of life, much as we accept poverty or guns in our own time?

Washington at Mount Vernon, 1797, N. Currier, ca. 1852. (Library of Congress, LC-DIG-pga-10101)

African slavery was a part of the given landscape of his life, as familiar as breathing. As a young child, he lived on family farms that relied on enslaved labor, and his earliest memories would have included observation of his father and mother in their direct management and supervision of the enslaved. Slavery was not something to like or dislike; it simply was. His parents, his Bible, his church, his government, and his societal leaders all gave sanction to the institution of human slavery. He became a slaveholder at the age of eleven and owned enslaved workers until his death in 1799, when the majority of people witnessing his death scene were some of those enslaved workers.

The central question becomes when—and why—did George Washington evolve from a typical Virginia slaveholder into the only one of the founding fathers who devised a plan to free all of the enslaved workers he owned?

Clearly, the impact of the American Revolution and the antislavery beliefs of younger men whom he admired—Marquis de Lafayette,

Anti-slavery token, ca. 1795. (Mount Vernon Ladies' Association)

Alexander Hamilton, John Laurens, and David Humphreys—were crucial in this regard. The author of the best and most comprehensive study of George Washington and slavery asserts, "During the conflict [the War of Independence] his views on slavery were radically altered, evidence that he truly believed the wartime rhetoric about freedom and liberty."[7] Certainly, the General was well aware of the call that it was time for America to act on the principles of the Declaration of Independence: "that all mankind came from the hand of the Creator equally free."

Intellectually, Washington would have agreed with the assertion that slavery was an evil which must be eradicated. Yet, my sense after studying this issue is that George Washington never *viscerally* felt slavery's evil. Although his experience during the war had exposed Washington to a larger world of egalitarian values, he continued to think like a typical Virginia slave owner in his private role as master of Mount Vernon.[8] This key insight can help us better understand many of his actions in the period from the American Revolution until the time of his death.

That Washington never viscerally felt slavery's evil is most clearly illustrated by an examination of his dealings regarding runaway slaves, which were consistent throughout his life. A man viscerally opposed to slavery would have been at least somewhat sympathetic to bondsmen and bondswomen who tried to escape from the system. Washington never expressed any sympathy for runaways—either his own or those belonging to other planters.

From George Washington's perspective, an enslaved laborer who ran away was guilty of the gravest betrayal of his or her presumed duty. During the War of Independence, large numbers of enslaved workers, estimated to be about six thousand souls, attempted to flee to freedom, particularly during the Yorktown Campaign in 1781. Authorities made concerted efforts to return recaptured fugitives to their owners after the British surrender.

In his General Orders of October 25, 1783, General Washington declared:

> It having been represented that many Negroes and Mulattoes the property of Citizens of these States have concealed themselves on board the Ships in the harbor, that some still continue to attach themselves to British Officers and that others have attempted to impose themselves upon the officers of the French and American Armies as Freemen and to make their escapes in that manner. In order to prevent their succeeding in such practices All Officers of the Allied Army and other persons of every denomination concerned are directed not to suffer any such negroes or mulattoes to be retained in their Service but on the contrary to cause them to be delivered to the Guards which will be establish'd for their reception at one of the Redoubts in York and another in Gloucester.[9]

The General's response to a letter from his friend William Fitzhugh is telling. Fitzhugh wrote Washington in the aftermath of the victory at Yorktown requesting that Washington ask Lieutenant General de Grasse whether five of Fitzhugh's laborers—believed to have sailed away with the French fleet—might be recovered. Promptly upon receiving Fitzhugh's letter, Washington wrote de Grasse, explaining that it would be "a very great favor if your Excellency will direct them to be sent back by any Vessel coming either to Virginia or Maryland."[10] Washington then forwarded to Fitzhugh a copy of his letter to de Grasse, adding his hope that it produces "the effect you wish it to have, with Count de Grasse."[11]

Runaways directly impacted George Washington. When the British warship HMS *Savage* dropped anchor near Mount Vernon in 1781, seventeen of the General's enslaved workers, fourteen men and three women, absconded with the hope of gaining their freedom. (They are all listed by name, age, and condition in a report to Washington from his cousin and overseer, Lund Washington.) Washington joined a group of slaveholders who hired a Fairfax neighbor to travel to New York City in search of fugitive slaves. Eventually, approximately half of the fugitive Washington slaves were recovered.

The General had a contentious confrontation with General Guy Carleton, who presided over the British evacuation of New York City in 1783 as the war drew to a close. Washington objected to British plans to take with them those slaves who had served with the British army, arguing that the provisional articles of peace prohibited such removal. According to the account of one British participant, Washington had demanded the return of the escaped slaves, "with all the Grossness and Ferocity of a Captain of Banditti."[12] It is clear that Washington had a hard streak in his personality. Callousness probably figured in his success as a revolutionary leader, but it could also manifest itself in unattractive ways.

A little-known episode strengthens the argument that Washington was unsympathetic to runaways whether they belonged to him or not. He shared the following story with his friend and former aide, James McHenry: "One of the Servants who accompany's my Overseer, belongs to the Honble William Drayton of Charleston So. Ca. This Gentn spent a day or two here on his return from New York, and at Dumfries (proceeding on) the above fellow run away from him & came here. He goes to Baltimore under the impression of assisting in bringing the Jack & Mules home, but the real design of sending him there is to have him shipped for Charleston."[13] Apparently, Washington's effort at duplicity was not immediately successful because the unnamed individual in question managed to run away after arriving in Baltimore—only to be eventually returned to his master about six months later.

One of the best-known and most disturbing vignettes concerning George Washington and his runaway enslaved workers involves his reaction to the escape of one of his house servants, Ona Judge, who served Martha Washington in much the same manner as William Lee served the General. The Washingtons simply could not fathom why Oney, as they called her, would run off. In Washington's words, she left "without the least provocation."[14] From his perspective, her flight appeared to be ungrateful behavior on the part of a young woman whom he and his wife had treated more "like a child than a servant."

The president's protracted negotiations to retrieve Ona, extending even to the year of his death, do not reflect well on him. Having learned that she was living in Portsmouth, New Hampshire, the president used the full force of his influence, improperly if truth be told, to hunt her down. He wrote privately to his secretary of the treasury, Oliver Wolcott, asking him to enlist the aid of the customs collector at Portsmouth, Joseph Whipple, "to seize, and put her on board a vessel" bound either for Philadelphia or Alexandria, for which he would pay all costs.[15] Such action violated the provisions of the Fugitive Slave Law which George Washington had quickly signed into law in 1793, again demonstrating his lack of sympathy for runaways. The law required that the slave owner or his representative appear before a magistrate and provide evidence of ownership before attempting to transport a fugitive slave to another state.[16]

His effort fell through because Washington was fearful of drawing unwelcome attention to the incident. New Hampshire was strongly antislavery, and Washington was afraid that if the removal took place in public, it would damage his much-cherished reputation. Even so, he did not let the matter drop. In the final year of his life, on learning that his nephew Burwell Bassett was going to Portsmouth, Washington made a final attempt to reclaim Ona, explaining to Bassett that such an action would please his aunt. That plan was also thwarted, and Ona ended up outliving her former enslaver by nearly fifty years, dying an impoverished but free and literate woman in 1849.[17]

Fear of losing some of his most valued house servants led to one of the most troublesome incidents of Washington's presidency. He took extraordinary covert measures to prevent his house domestics from securing the legal rights that were theirs under a Pennsylvania law automatically freeing slaves after six months of residence in that state. Washington secretly ordered his private secretary, Tobias Lear, to game the statutory calendar, briefly relocating some of his slaves back in Virgina, thus invalidating their right to claim their freedom. "I wish to have it accomplished under pretext that may deceive both them and the Public," Washington wrote.[18] In this same troubling letter, Washington voiced doubt that, if the slaves were in fact freed, "they would be benefitted by the change," but admitted that "the idea of freedom might be too great a temptation for them to resist."

One reason that Washington had little patience with runaways was that he held a patriarchal view toward the institution of slavery. The essence of patriarchalism was its insistence on the existence of reciprocal obligations and duties between master and servant. The master would provide care for his dependents, who in return would work for him. Washington's language on this point is very clear: "It has always been my aim to feed and cloath them well, and be careful of them in sickness; in return I expect such labor as they ought to render."[19] In a letter to an overseer in 1789, he ordered that his "people" were to be "at their work as soon as it is light, work till it is dark, and be diligent while they are it. . . . Lost labor is never to be regained. . . . Every labourer (male or female) [should do] as much in the 24 hours as their strength without endangering the health, or constitution will allow."[20] Washington actually felt he often suffered from the arrangement. When bondman Isaac's cabin burned down, Washington told his overseer to inform Isaac, "I sustain injury enough by their idleness—they need not add to it by their carelessness."[21]

What if the workers didn't keep their end of the bargain, which Washington felt was fair? His answer was clear. If the workers would not fulfill "their duty by fair means, they must be compelled to do it."[22] His insistence on "compelling" his bondsmen led to regrettable blots on the historical record of George Washington as a slave owner. Washington inadvertently confessed to his close friend Bryan Fairfax that he ruled his workers with "arbitrary sway."[23] Henrietta Liston, the perceptive wife of the British ambassador, while acknowledging the president's consistent control of his passions on public occasions, noted that "in private and particularly with his Servants, its violence sometimes broke out."[24] The Englishman Richard Parkinson was shocked at the way the president spoke to his enslaved workers—"as differently as if he had been quite another man, or had been in anger."[25] It was as if the General were once again disciplining raw soldiers. And, as with raw troops, Washington believed that leniency could be counterproductive.

Theft was a constant and aggravating problem at George Washington's Mount Vernon estate. At one point Washington ordered that most of the dogs belonging to his enslaved workers there be shot because they served as sentinels for night raids to pilfer plantation stores. He further ordered that "if any Negro [still] presumes under any pretense whatsoever, to preserve, or bring one into the family . . . he shall be severely punished, and the dog hanged."[26]

There are many documented cases of Washington authorizing the use of the whip at Mount Vernon to keep his enslaved workers in line. The best-known case involved an enslaved seamstress, Charlotte. Perceiving Charlotte as impudent, overseer Anthony Whitting gave her "a very good whipping" and promised he was "determined to lower her Spirit or skin her Back."[27] George Washington wrote back that he considered Whitting's treatment of Charlotte to be "very proper."

"If She, or any other of the Servants will not do their duty by fair means, or are impertinent, correction (as the only alternative) must be administered."[28] In a quirk of circumstance, Charlotte was present in the room when Washington died.

While there is no record of Washington himself ever whipping any of his enslaved workers, there are at least a couple of examples documenting his use of force when displeased.[29] Isaac described how, when his tree-felling displeased the proprietor, the General, without a word, "gave me such a slap on the side of my head that I whirled round like a top and before I knew where I was Master was gone."

Lawrence Washington, Washington's nephew and farm manager, noted that whenever a servant brought the General a pair of boots, he would carefully examine the footwear. If they were in satisfactory condition, he put the boots on. If not, Lawrence recounted, "the servant got them about his head but without the Genl. betraying any excitement beyond the effort of the moment."[30]

Despite such troubling facts, one cannot read Washington's private correspondence and reach any other conclusion than that, in the years following the War of Independence, Washington became increasingly antislavery on an intellectual level and wished for a way to abolish the practice. Among many such quotes: "I can only say that there is not a man living who wishes more sincerely than I do, to see a plan adopted for this abolition of [slavery]."[31] "Not only do I pray for it on the score of human dignity, but I can clearly foresee that nothing but the rooting out of slavery can perpetuate the existence of our union."[32]

It is important to note that these and other similar quotes are all from his private correspondence.[33] Washington made no public statement criticizing the institution of slavery prior to the publication of his will.

Why, if Washington saw the evil of slavery and feared that it threatened the Union's existence, did he not use his unparalleled prestige as the hero of American independence to try to address the crisis by explicitly warning his countrymen of the dangers of perpetuating slavery as an economic pillar? Why, on the most pressing moral question facing the nation, did its greatest leader not lead? Should he be held culpable for a dereliction of duty? François Furstenberg, in a particularly thoughtful essay on George Washington and slavery, called Washington "The Father of the Nation: who could not confront the hardest of realities, who ambivalently bequeathed slavery onto his descendants—and who left us with a legacy we still wrestle with today."[34] Is that a fair criticism?

There are two points to consider: Why did George Washington act as he did, and was he justified in his decision? While I will argue that one central factor kept Washington from publicly attacking slavery, there were at least two other reasons that made it easier for Washington to decide against taking direct action.

One was that his own life and livelihood were increasingly enmeshed with slavery. In an important new book on Washington and slavery, Bruce Ragsdale demonstrates that Washington's various records regarding farming at Mount Vernon provide the most detailed documentation of his engagement with slavery and his very conflicted attitude toward the practice.[35] Ragsdale mines the records well and demonstrates that while privately calling for abolition, Washington simultaneously was increasing his reliance on enslaved laborers in every aspect of the new and complicated course of British husbandry he was establishing at Mount Vernon. Simply put, he could not engineer the advances he envisioned at Mount Vernon unless he commanded a large slave labor force. Thus, his path on slavery continued to veer between principle and self-interest.[36] As Joseph Ellis writes, "His conscience and more self-interested calculations were entangled in his own mind."[37]

Second, because he did not viscerally oppose slavery, Washington simply did not identify at a deep emotional level with the plight of the enslaved. Note his reaction to a memorial by Quakers presented to Congress and to the Friends' calls to end slavery. He called their memorial "an ill-judged piece of business" and "a great waste of time."[38]

He complained that the Quakers were stirring up unnecessary trouble between owner and slave: "But when slaves [who] are happy and contented with their present masters, are tampered with and seduced to leave them; when masters are taken unawares by these practices, when a conduct of this sort begets discontent on one side and resentment on the other . . . it is oppression in such a case, and not humanity in any, because it introduces more evils than it can cure."[39]

Even if those two factors were not at play, George Washington would have acted exactly the same way concerning slavery. Why? Because he firmly believed that if the issue of abolishing slavery were pushed, the country would dissolve. Almost certainly, Abraham Lincoln's words on the eve of the Civil War well expressed Washington's philosophy: "What I do about slavery, and the colored race, I do because I believe it helps to save the Union; and I forbear because I do not believe it would help to save the Union."

Preserving and strengthening the Union was always Washington's guiding star. Moving against slavery would put the Union in mortal jeopardy. Ever a realist, he believed any public statement would be ineffective and would undermine his own authority and credibility. Ending slavery was not a cause that Washington would ever risk a great deal to promote. Certainly, he would not do so when he concluded that any such move would not free the slaves but would destroy his beloved Union. It is worth noting that slavery is not even referenced in Washington's famous Farewell Address. It was simply too divisive a topic to bring up.

If that assessment is accurate, and I believe that it is, it is not fair to say that Washington bequeathed slavery to his descendants. That was the reality he had to face. For the reasons stated above, Washington chose not to use his great prestige to publicly attack the institution of slavery, but he used that same prestige to firmly establish a permanent Union for the United States with the tools to do so later.

Ultimately, when George Washington decided to comment publicly and forcefully on the issue of slavery, he did so in his will, which he knew would be widely reprinted and discussed.[40] (Indeed, it was published as a pamphlet in thirteen editions in 1800 alone.)[41] His will set up a plan to free all the enslaved workers to whom he held title; by law, he could not free those belonging to his wife and the Custis estate.

His growing recognition that slavery was not a viable economic system figured in his decision. In economic terms, slavery simply did not work. And Washington clearly recognized that slavery violated the tenets of American liberty. That said, I believe that the main reason he spoke out against slavery had to do with his "posterity project."[42] Historian Joseph Ellis stated it well: "He knew that posterity was watching and freeing his slaves would help clear his legacy of the major impediment to his secular immortality. Doing the right thing for his slaves became imperative because it also meant doing the right thing for his historical reputation."[43] George Washington very much wanted to be on the right side of history, and he hoped this dramatic action would help ensure that result.

Significantly, in his will, Washington went beyond simply arranging to free the children of his enslaved workers. Orphan offspring, or those whose parents were unable or unwilling to provide for them, would be bound as apprentices until age twenty-five with the proviso that their masters and mistresses were to teach them to read and write. This surprising—at the time almost shocking—provision was in harmony with what Washington had earlier told his would-be biographer, David Humphreys. Washington said that to be able "to lay a foundation to prepare the rising generation for a destiny different from that in which they were born, afforded some satisfaction to my mind, and could not I hoped be displeasing to the justice of the Creator."[44] To drive home the importance of his decision, the president particularly enjoined his executors "to see that this clause respecting Slaves, and *every* part thereof be *religiously* fulfilled. . . . without evasion, neglect or delay."[45] Supporters quickly concluded that Washington's deathbed emancipation was the culmination of a lifetime commitment to freedom for all people.[46] It is important to note, however, that the will offers no prescription by which Washington's fellow slaveholders might move toward emancipation. Washington, it seems, was more intent on erasing the charge of "slaveholder" from his reputation than on putting that reputation to work eradicating the peculiar institution.[47]

No doubt, Washington, an elitist by nature and circumstance, felt an ingrained sense of racial superiority toward African Americans, but it did not lead to Negrophobia. Nowhere in any of his writings, public or private, does he indicate support for the widely held view that colonization was the only satisfactory way to deal with the problem of how to eventually free the enslaved. He never accepted the racist belief that Blacks were congenitally unfit for freedom and that emancipation would therefore lead to chaos and anarchy. Washington "tended to regard the condition of the black population as a product of nurture rather than nature."[48] He also recognized and recommended instances of Black achievement, with his wartime letter to the poet Phillis Wheatley being perhaps the best-known example.[49]

Washington fully anticipated that freed slaves would remain in Virginia as self-supporting and independent people. The will is clearest regarding this matter in the passage in which Washington extends to the Black children he manumits the same legal protections accorded dependent white children.[50]

Inevitably, George Washington's historical stature is somewhat diminished by the "grating chain of racism and slavery that snaked through the new republic," entwining him and shaping his views on slavery and race. Nevertheless, in freeing the people he had enslaved, he proved to be the most celebrated defender of liberty, and he paid the "last greatest debt he owed to his honor."[51]

ACKNOWLEDGMENTS

Writing this book has boosted my confidence regarding the future. So many nice, smart, and talented people happily shared their time and expertise to bring this project to completion, in many cases receiving nothing more than a thank-you.

My friend and editor Michael Dolan deserves a special shoutout. Mike has the talent to significantly improve my prose without in any way changing the points I want to make.

Many scholars, including the two unnamed readers of the original draft, shared their expertise to help produce the final product. Bill Ferraro, an editor at the George Washington Papers, not only read the entire manuscript but also steered me to as yet unpublished material and helped me track down a few endnotes when I ran into blank walls. Joe Ellis was not only kind enough to give me access to his forthcoming book, *Realities and Regrets,* but also allowed me to quote from that work. Rereading my manuscript, I realized that I quoted Joe more than anyone else. That is because we tend to see George Washington in the same way, and Joe is a master wordsmith.

Mary Thompson, Bruce Ragsdale, and John Ferling, all top scholars in their respective areas, read my section on Washington and slavery and strengthened my essay on that very important and controversial topic. Rick Brookhiser read an early draft of the manuscript, made helpful suggestions, and encouraged me to pursue the work through to publication.

Lynn McIntosh, a dear friend and excellent photographer, spent a great deal of time producing the photo for the book jacket.

Family members also played important roles. Without my beloved wife Marlene's encouragement, I would not have started on the journey. Diana Henriques, prize-winning journalist, read the draft and made helpful suggestions. My sister Judy Pierce, whom I call "Mistress of the Comma," gave the work two very careful readings, catching mistakes that others missed. My brilliant son Gregg, a psychology professor at James Madison University and an expert on human nature, helped me better grasp the various forces that drove George Washington.

Dawn Bonner represents Mount Vernon at its best. She is friendly, knowledgeable, helpful, and very prompt. We ultimately decided to use twenty illustrations in the book, and she helped find most of them.

I can't emphasize enough what a pleasure it was to work with the University of Virgina Press, starting with Nadine Zimmerli, who was appointed editor in chief right at the time they were deciding whether to publish my manuscript. Despite her profuse duties, Nadine always found time to coach me and help me through the procedure to win approval. Then she found two wonderful graduate students, William Nichols and Kristen Stewart, to help me with key tasks I don't like to do and am not very good at. William wrangled my 378 endnotes into the proper form. Kristen succeeded in negotiating permission for all the desired illustrations, several of which required deft prodding. She was a joy to work with. I enthusiastically rank Ellen Satrom, managing editor and editorial, design, and production director, first in timely responding to my various queries and for keeping me on task, always in a friendly and supportive way. I could tell immediately that my copy editor, Susan Murray, was a true professional whom I could easily work with as we shared a goal—to make the finished product as good as possible. I want to particularly thank Cecilia Sorochin for not following my suggestion and instead creating a cover design that seems to please everyone who views it. Thanks also go to Mary Kate Maco, Jason Coleman, Clayton Butler, and the marketing team at the press for helping get the word out about the book. Readers who use the index will be grateful that Enid Zafran prepared it, so as to be useful in a way that many indexes are not.

Finally, I wish to acknowledge the very friendly but largely anonymous listeners at Colonial Williamsburg who came to my talks on the seven stages of George Washington's life and responded in such a way that encouraged me to share my work with a larger audience.

NOTES

Abbreviations

FOL	Founders Online
MVLA	Mount Vernon Ladies' Association
PGWCF	*Confederation Series, The Papers of George Washington*
PGWCL	*Colonial Series, The Papers of George Washington*
PGWP	*Presidential Series, The Papers of George Washington*
PGWRT	*Retirement Series, The Papers of George Washington*
PGWRV	*Revolutionary Series, The Papers of George Washington*

Note: Most of George Washington's correspondence is available both on Founders Online (https://founders.archives.gov) and in the printed volumes of *The Papers of George Washington* (published by the University of Virginia Press in the series listed above). My decision on which one to cite was determined by which source I used for the quotations.

Introduction

1. For a detailed look at the national mourning following Washington's death, see Gerald E. Kahler, *The Long Farewell: Americans Mourn the Death of George Washington* (University of Virginia Press, 2008).
2. Quoted in Mary Thompson, *The Only Unavoidable Subject of Regret: George Washington, Slavery and the Enslaved Community at Mount Vernon* (University of Virginia Press, 2019), 293–94.
3. Quoted in Thompson, *The Only Unavoidable Subject of Regret*, 293–94.
4. John Rhodehamel, *George Washington: The Wonder of the Age* (Yale University Press, 2017), 9.
5. The classic treatment of this subject is Douglass Adair, "Fame and the Founding Fathers," in *Fame and the Founding Fathers: Essays by Douglass Adair*, ed. T. Colbourn (Institute of Early American History and Culture, 1974).

1. Young Man on the Make

1. Rhodehamel, *Wonder of the Age*, 13.
2. *PGWCL* 1:45–46.
3. For more on their relationship, see Peter R. Henriques, *First and Always: A New Portrait of George Washington* (University of Virginia Press, 2020). See also Martha Saxton, *The Widow Washington: The Life of Mary Washington* (Farrar, Straus and Giroux, 2019).
4. Ron Chernow, *Washington: A Life* (Penguin, 2010), 11.
5. Douglas Southall Freeman, *George Washington: A Biography*, 7 vols. (Scribner, 1948–57), 2:384.
6. George Washington Parke Custis, *Recollections and Private Memoirs of Washington* (New York, 1860), 130.
7. Paul K. Longmore, *The Invention of George Washington* (University of Virginia Press, 1999), 1. Now nearly thirty years old, it was a groundbreaking book leading to a better understanding of George Washington. All Washington scholars are much in his debt.
8. For a detailed examination of this trial, see Peter R. Henriques, "Major Lawrence Washington versus the Reverend Charles Green: A Case Study of the Parson versus the Squire," *Virginia Magazine of History and Biography* 100, no. 2 (1992): 233–64.
9. GW to John Augustine Washington, 28 May 1755, FOL.
10. GW to Robert Dinwiddie, 17 September 1757, FOL.
11. I wish to credit Dr. Jack Warren for this insight.
12. Peter Stark, *Young Washington: How Wilderness and War Forged America's Founding Father* (HarperCollins, 2018), 49. This is the best available work on Washington's early years.
13. Quote in James Thomas Flexner, *George Washington: The Forge of Experience, 1732–1775* (Little, Brown, 1965), 191–92. Richard Brookhiser

pointed out to me that there is some doubt as to the authenticity of this quote, although it is consistent with other, less detailed descriptions of Washington.

14. Quoted in *PGWCL* 1:57.
15. Stark, *Young Washington,* 49.
16. Stark, *Young Washington,* 74.
17. George Washington's journal, quoted in *George Washington's Diaries: An Abridgement,* ed. Dorothy Twohig (University of Virginia Press, 1999), 23.
18. GW to Richard Corbin, February–March 1754, *PGWCL* 1:70.
19. Thomas A. Lewis, *For King and Country: The Maturing of George Washington, 1748–1760* (HarperCollins, 1993), xv.
20. GW to Robert Dinwiddie, 9 March 1754, FOL.

2. A Frustrating War and a Successful Marriage

1. I am greatly indebted to Guthrie Sayen's excellent dissertation "A Complete Gentleman: The Making of George Washington, 1732–1775" (PhD diss., University of Connecticut, 1988).
2. Stark, *Young Washington,* 5.
3. Lewis, *For King and Country,* 133.
4. Quoted in Longmore, *Invention of George Washington,* 24.
5. David Preston, *Braddock's Defeat: The Battle of the Monongahela and the Road to Revolution* (Oxford University Press, 2015), 352.
6. Quoted in Stark, *Young Washington,* 126.
7. GW to John Augustine Washington, 31 May 1754, *PGWCL* 1:118.
8. GW to Robert Dinwiddie, 3 June 1754, *PGWCL* 1:124.
9. Most of this is quoted in Joseph J. Ellis, *His Excellency: George Washington* (Knopf, 2004), 17–18.
10. GW to unknown recipient, ca. 1757, *PGWCL* 1:169–70.
11. Invoice, 23 October 1754, *PGWCL* 1:217.
12. GW to William Fitzhugh, 15 November 1754, FOL.
13. GW to Sally Cary Fairfax, 25 September 1758, *PGWCL* 6:42.
14. GW to John Augustine Washington, 18 July 1755, *PGWCL* 1:343.
15. GW to John Augustine Washington, 18 July 1755, *PGWCL* 1:342. The quote is often given as "Providence protected me beyond all human expectation," and is cited as a letter to Governor Dinwiddie of the same date. In that letter, Washington actually wrote, "I luckily escaped without a wound."
16. Stark, *Young Washington,* 287.
17. GW to Robert Dinwiddie, 10 March 1757, FOL.
18. GW to Richard Washington, 15 April 1757, FOL.
19. GW to Robert Dinwiddie, 22 April 1756, FOL.
20. I wish to credit Joseph Ellis with this insight.
21. GW to Robert Dinwiddie, 19 December 1756, FOL.
22. GW to Lord Loudoun, 10 January 1757, *PGWCL* 4:79–90.

23. Flexner, *Forge of Experience,* 175.
24. GW to Richard Washington, 20 October 1761, *PGWCL* 7:80.
25. GW to Thomas Gage, 12 April 1758, FOL.
26. GW to John Robinson, 1 September 1758, *PGWCL* 5:433.
27. John Forbes to Henry Bouquet, 4 September 1758; quoted in *PGWCL* 5:377n2.
28. GW to John Robinson, 1 September 1758, *PGWCL* 5:433.
29. GW to Sally Cary Fairfax, 25 September 1758, *PGWCL* 6:42. Robert L. O'Connell argues the most likely explanation is that they were briefly lovers (*Revolutionary: George Washington at War* [Random House, 2019], 42).
30. The story is well told in Stark, *Young Washington,* 386–88.
31. Quoted in Lewis, *For King and Country,* 273.
32. Quoted in Flexner, *Forge of Experience,* 222.
33. For more detail on their relationship, see Peter R. Henriques, *Realistic Visionary: A Portrait of George Washington* (University of Virginia Press, 2008), chap. 9.
34. GW to Richard Washington, 20 September 1759, FOL.
35. David O. Stewart, *George Washington: The Political Rise of America's Founding Father* (Dutton Books, 2021), 90.
36. O'Connell, *Revolutionary,* 47.

3. From Loyal Virginia Gentleman to Rebel Chieftain

1. GW to David Humphreys, 25 July 1785, FOL.
2. This topic is explored at length in the prize-winning book by Kevin J. Hayes, *George Washington: A Life in Books* (Oxford University Press, 2017).
3. Quoted in Sayen, "A Complete Gentleman," 20. Much of the next section is drawn from this fine work.
4. Paul Longmore develops this theme very effectively in *The Invention of George Washington,* and I draw on him for parts of this section.
5. GW to James Wood, 28 July 1758, FOL.
6. GW to Van Swearingen, 15 May 1761, *PGWCL* 7:43.
7. GW to Willliam Ramsay, 29 January 1769, FOL.
8. GW uses the term in a letter to Presley Nevill, 16 June 1794, FOL.
9. Ellis, *His Excellency,* 46.
10. See Linda Colley, *Britons: Forging the Nation 1707–1837* (Yale University Press, 2009).
11. GW to Robert Dinwiddie, 10 March 1757, FOL.
12. Rhodehamel, *Wonder of the Age,* 95.
13. This paragraph draws heavily from Ellis, *His Excellency,* 48–51.
14. See Chernow, *Washington,* 176.
15. GW to George Mason, 5 April 1769, *PGWCL* 8:28.
16. Arthur Lee to GW, 15 June 1777, PGWRV 10:43–44.

17. GW to Bryan Fairfax, 24 August 1774, FOL.
18. GW to George William Fairfax, 31 May 1775, *PGWCL* 10:368.
19. GW to John Augustine Washington, 25 March 1775, *PGWCL* 10:308.
20. John Adams, Diary, 31 August 1774.
21. Benjamin Rush to Thomas Rushton, 29 October 1775, *Letters of Benjamin Rush*, 2 vols., ed L. H. Butterfield (Princeton University Press, 1951), 1:92.
22. Quoted in Sayen, "A Complete Gentleman," 204.
23. Quoted in Sayen, "A Complete Gentleman," 205.
24. This theme is developed in Stephen Brumwell, *George Washington: Gentleman Warrior* (Quercus, 2013).
25. GW to Martha Washington, 18 June 1775, FOL.
26. GW to Sally Cary Fairfax, 25 September 1758, *PGWCL* 6:42.
27. Stewart, *George Washington*, 202.
28. I wish to credit John Rhodehamel for this insight.
29. William Shakespeare, *Julius Caesar*, act 4, scene 2.
30. GW to Bryan Fairfax, 20 January 1799, FOL.
31. John Adams to John Trumbull, 27 July 1805, FOL.
32. Jonathan Horn, *Washington's End: The Final Years and Forgotten Struggle* (Scribner, 2020), 104. This is the best book on Washington's final years.
33. Ellis, *His Excellency*, 70–71.
34. Chernow, *Washington*, 188.
35. Stewart, *George Washington*, 206.
36. O'Connell, *Revolutionary*, xxvii.
37. Quoted in Richard Norton Smith, *Patriarch: George Washington and the New American Nation* (Mariner Books, 1997), 3.
38. Quoted in James Thomas Flexner, *George Washington in the American Revolution, 1775–1783* (Little, Brown, 1968), 9.

4. America's Cincinnatus

1. Address to New York Provisional Congress, 26 June 1775, FOL.
2. John Adams to Elbridge Gerry, 18 June 1775, FOL.
3. Carol Cadou, "Silver Swords to Silk Waistcoats," in *The George Washington Collection: Fine and Decorative Arts at Mount Vernon*, ed. Carol Cadou (Hudson Hills, 2006), 213.
4. Quoted in Paul Leicester Ford, *The True George Washington* (Philadelphia, 1896), 39.
5. GW to Lund Washington, 20 August 1775, FOL.
6. See Rick Atkinson, *The British Are Coming: The War for America, Lexington to Princeton, 1775–1777* (Henry Holt, 2019), 389–91. The Tench Tilghman quote is from Edward G. Lengel, *General George Washington: A Military Life* (Random House, 2005).
7. GW to Lund Washington, 30 September 1776, FOL.

8. GW to Lund Washington, 30 September 1776, FOL.
9. GW to Samuel Washington, 18 December 1776, FOL.
10. GW to Richard Henry Lee, 29 August 1775, PGWRV 1:372–76, quote on 375.
11. GW to Jonathan Trumbull, Jr., 30 August 1799, *PGWRT* 4:275–76, quote on 276.
12. GW to Benjamin Harrison, 18–30 March 1778, FOL.
13. Email from William Ferraro, an editor of the University of Virginia's *Papers of George Washington,* to the author. I wish to gratefully acknowledge Professor Ferraro's help with this work.
14. GW to Samuel Huntington, 4 April 1781, FOL.
15. GW to Basaleel Howe, 9 November 1783, FOL.
16. Marcus Cunliffe, *George Washington: Man and Monument* (Little, Brown, 1958), 145.
17. Robert Morris to GW, 27 February 1777, FOL.
18. Joseph Addison, *Cato,* act 1, scene 2.
19. Ellis, *His Excellency,* 74.
20. This paragraph is drawn from William M. Ferraro, "George Washington's Mind," in *A Companion to George Washington,* ed. Edward Lengel (Wiley-Blackwell, 2012), 548.
21. GW to James Madison, 3 December 1784, FOL.
22. Joseph J. Ellis, *American Creation: Triumphs and Tragedies at the Founding of the Republic* (Knopf, 2007), 67.
23. GW to John Hancock, 25 September 1776, FOL.
24. GW to John Hancock, 25 September 1776, FOL.
25. GW to John Hancock, 20 December 1776, FOL.
26. GW to William Woodford, 10 November 1775, FOL.
27. GW to John Sullivan, 25 July 1777, FOL.
28. GW to Joseph Reed, 1 April 1776, FOL.
29. Quoted in Albert Bushnell Hart, ed., *Honor to George Washington and Reading about George Washington* (United States George Washington Bicentennial Commission, 1932), 111.
30. James Thomas Flexner, *Washington: The Indispensable Man* (Little, Brown, 1974), 110.
31. O'Connell, *Revolutionary,* 165.
32. Quoted in Atkinson, *The British Are Coming,* 497.
33. O'Connell, *Revolutionary,* 149.
34. This is a central theme of O'Connell, *Revolutionary.*
35. Rhodehamel, *Wonder of the Age,* 182.
36. Quoted in John Ferling, *Whirlwind: The American Revolution and the War That Won It* (Bloomsbury, 2015), 179.
37. David Richard Palmer, *George Washington's Military Genius* (Regnery, 2012), 78.
38. The best treatment of this very important event is William M. Fowler, *An American Crisis: George Washington and the Dangerous Two Years After Yorktown, 1781–1783* (Walker Books, 2013).

39. Quoted in Chernow, *Washington*, 435.
40. Fowler, *An American Crisis*, 186.
41. Stewart, *George Washington*, 95.
42. Thomas Paine, *Common Sense*, 1.
43. I wish to credit Edward Lengel with this analogy.
44. GW to Samuel Washington, 18 December 1776, FOL.
45. GW to Robert Morris, 25 December 1776, FOL.
46. GW to John Hancock, 20 December 1776, FOL.
47. GW to Horatio Gates, 14 December 1776, FOL.
48. Entitled *George Washington Crossing the Delaware River*, this gigantic painting, measuring roughly 12 feet by 21 feet, is housed in the New York Metropolitan Museum of Art.
49. Atkinson, *The British Are Coming*, 117.
50. Atkinson, *The British Are Coming*, 512.
51. O'Connell, *Revolutionary*, 159.
52. David Hackett Fischer, *Washington's Crossing* (Oxford University Press, 2004), 272.
53. GW to John Hancock, 5 January 1777, FOL.
54. Atkinson, *The British Are Coming*, 546.
55. O'Connell, *Revolutionary*, 163.
56. Fischer, *Washington's Crossing*, 362.
57. O'Connell, *Revolutionary*, 164.
58. Atkinson, *The British Are Coming*, 553.
59. Fischer, *Washington's Crossing*, 95.
60. For the importance of this decision, see Elizabeth A. Fenn, *Pox Americana: The Great Smallpox Epidemic of 1775–82* (Hill and Wang, 2002).
61. GW to James Varnum, 4 November 1777, FOL.
62. Quote by Benjamin Tallmadge. See Fowler, *An American Crisis*, 233.

5. Returning to the Fray

1. Francis D. Cogliano, *A Revolutionary Friendship: Washington, Jefferson, and the American Republic* (Harvard University Press, 2024), 248.
2. François Furstenberg, *In the Name of the Father: Washington's Legacy, Slavery, and the Making of a Nation* (Penguin, 2006), 65.
3. Garry Wills, *Cincinnatus: George Washington and the Enlightenment* (Doubleday, 1984), 13. For a more detailed discussion, see *The Papers of George Washington Newsletter*, no. 12 (Spring 2011): 9–10.
4. Ellis, *His Excellency*, 146.
5. Quoted in Gilbert Chinard, *George Washington as the French Knew Him: A Collection of Texts* (Princeton University Press, 1940), 69.
6. Quoted in Gordon S. Wood, "The Greatness of George Washington," in *George Washington Reconsidered*, ed. Don Higginbotham (University of Virginia Press, 2001), 311.

7. Gordon S. Wood, *The Radicalism of the American Revolution* (Vintage Books, 1993), 206.
8. GW to Marquis de Lafayette, 1 February 1784, FOL.
9. GW to Marquis de Lafayette, 28 May 1788, FOL.
10. John Ferling, *The Ascent of George Washington: The Hidden Political Genius of an American Icon* (Bloomsbury, 2009), 368.
11. This paragraph is drawn from Glenn A. Phelps, *George Washington and American Constitutionalism* (University of Kansas Press, 1993), 68.
12. GW to Benjamin Harrison, 18 January 1784, FOL.
13. GW to the States, 8 June 1783, FOL.
14. GW to James Madison, 5 November 1786, *PGWCF* 4:332.
15. GW to John Jay, 18 May 1786, *PGWCF* 4:55–56.
16. GW to Henry Knox, 26 December 1786, *PGWCF* 4:484.
17. GW to John Jay, 18 May 1786, *PGWCF* 4:56.
18. GW to John Jay, 15 August 1786, *PGWCF* 4:212.
19. The quote is from John Milton's *Samson Agonistes*.
20. GW to John Jay, 15 August 1786, *PGWCF* 4:213.
21. GW to John Jay, 15 August 1786, *PGWCF* 4:213.
22. GW to John Jay, 18 May 1786, *PGWCF* 4:56.
23. GW to Henry Knox, 8 March 1787, *PGWCF* 5:74 (emphasis added).
24. GW to John Jay, 18 May 1786, *PGWCF* 4:55.
25. GW to Henry Knox, 8 March 1787, *PGWCF* 5:74.
26. Henry Knox to GW, 19 March 1787, *PGWCF* 5:97.
27. GW to Henry Knox, 3 February 1787, *PGWCF* 5:9.
28. James Madison's role in convincing GW to attend the convention is explored in Stuart Leibiger, *Founding Friendship: George Washington, James Madison, and the Creation of the American Republic* (University of Virginia Press, 1999), chap. 3.
29. Rhodehamel, *Wonder of the Age,* 203.
30. Horn, *Washington's End,* 108.
31. GW to James Madison, 31 March 1787, *PGWCF* 5:116.
32. Edward J. Larson, *The Return of George Washington, 1783–1789* (Harper-Collins, 2014), 125.
33. James Thomas Flexner, *George Washington and the New Nation, 1783–1793* (Little, Brown, 1970), 118.
34. The delegate was Pierce Butler from Maryland (Flexner, *George Washington and the New Nation,* 134).
35. The bill for the libations and musicians may be accessed at https://www.quillproject.net/resources/resource_item/38/3109.
36. Quote by Alexander Donald (see *PGWCF* 5:425).
37. GW to Edward Newenham, 29 August 1788, *PGWCF* 6:488.
38. GW to Edmund Randolph, 8 January 1788, *PGWCF* 6:18.
39. GW to Catharine Macaulay Graham, 9 January 1790, FOL.
40. For an examination of the relationship between George Washington and George Mason, see Peter R. Henriques, "An Uneven Friendship," *Virginia Magazine of History and Biography* 97, no. 2 (1989): 185–204.

41. GW to Benjamin Lincoln, 2 April 1788, FOL.
42. GW to John Armstrong, 25 April 1788, FOL.
43. GW to Marquis de Lafayette, 28 May 1788, FOL.
44. Quoted in Larson, *Return of George Washington*, 179.
45. Quoted in Larson, *Return of George Washington*, 224.
46. Quoted in Flexner, *Indispensable Man*, 211.
47. GW to John Lathrop, 22 June 1788, FOL.
48. Gouverneur Morris to GW, 30 October 1787, FOL (emphasis in original).
49. AH to GW, *PGWCF* 6:444.
50. GW to Samuel Vaughn, 21 March 1789, FOL.
51. GW to William Gordon, 23 December 1788, FOL.
52. Smith, *Patriarch*, 250.
53. Cunliffe, *Man and Monument*, 137.
54. Elias Boudinot to GW, 6 April 1789, FOL.
55. GW to Benjamin Lincoln, 26 October 1788, FOL.
56. *Life of General Washington by David Humphreys*, ed. Rosemarie Zagarri (University of Georgia Press, 2006), xlix.
57. GW Diary Entry, 16 April 1789, FOL.
58. GW to Henry Knox, 1 April 1789, FOL.
59. T. H. Breen, *George Washington's Journey: The President Forges a Nation* (Simon & Schuster, 2017), 132.

6. Securing the Union

1. Peter R. Henriques, "'So Help Me God': A George Washington Myth That Should Be Discarded," https://www.historynewsnetwork.org/article/so-help-me-god-a-george-washington-myth-that-shoul.
2. George Washington to François-Joseph-Paul, Comte de Grasse-Tilly, 27 September 1781, FOL.
3. Smith, *Patriarch*, 54.
4. Ellis, *His Excellency*, 188.
5. Henry Knox to GW, 28 July 1788, FOL.
6. Cogliano, *Revolutionary Friendship*, 7.
7. Don Higginbotham, *George Washington: Uniting a Nation* (Rowman & Littlefield, 2004), 2.
8. Cogliano, *Revolutionary Friendship*, 196.
9. George Washington, *The Diaries of George Washington, 1748–1799*, ed. John Clement Fitzpatrick (Houghton Mifflin, 1925), 1771–85, 381.
10. Catharine Macaulay Graham to GW, 13 July 1785, *PGWCF* 3:116.
11. GW to Macaulay Graham, 9 January 1790, FOL (emphasis added).
12. GW to Macaulay Graham, 9 January 1790, FOL.
13. GW to David Stuart, 26 July 1789, FOL.
14. Stewart, *George Washington*, 157.
15. Quoted in Stewart, *George Washington*, 328.
16. Quoted in Stewart, *George Washington*, 213.

17. Gouverneur Morris to GW, 24 January 1790, FOL.
18. Wills, *Cincinnatus*, xxi.
19. T. H. Breen, *George Washington's Journey: The President Forges a New Nation* (Simon & Schuster, 2017), 25.
20. GW to David Humphreys, 20 July 1791, *PGWP* 8:359.
21. Phelps, *Washington and American Constitutionalism*, 81.
22. GW to Alexander Hamilton, 26 August 1792, FOL.
23. GW to Thomas Jefferson, 23 August 1792, FOL.
24. Thomas Jefferson's Memorandum of Conversations with GW, 1 March 1792, *PGWP* 10:5–10.
25. Thomas Jefferson to GW, 23 May 1792, *PGWP* 10:408–14.
26. Smith, *Patriarch*, 152.
27. Elizabeth Willing Powel to GW, 17 November 1792, FOL.
28. Rhodehamel, *Wonder of the Age*, 220.
29. Quoted in Smith, *Patriarch*, 165.
30. Joseph J. Ellis, *Founding Brothers: The Revolutionary Generation* (Knopf, 2000), 131.
31. GW to Henry Laurens, 14 November 1778, FOL. This theme is developed at length in Washington's Farewell Address (see Matthew Spalding and Patrick J. Garrity, *A Sacred Union of Citizens: George Washington's Farewell Address and the American Character* [Rowman & Littlefield, 1998]).
32. Quoted in Stewart, *George Washington*, 378.
33. Joseph J. Ellis, *American Sphinx: The Character of Thomas Jefferson* (Knopf, 1996), 157–61.
34. GW to Alexander Hamilton, 29 July 1795, FOL.
35. Quoted in Ron Chernow, *Alexander Hamilton* (Penguin, 2004), 486.
36. Quoted in Walter Stahr, *John Jay: Founding Father* (Bloomsbury Academic, 2005), 336.
37. GW, First Inaugural Address: Final Version, 30 April 1789, FOL.
38. GW to Gouverneur Morris, 22 December 1795, FOL.
39. Quoted in Cogliano, *Revolutionary Friendship*, 239.
40. Horn, *Washington's End*, 190.
41. James Monroe, *The Papers of James Monroe*, vol. 4: *Selected Correspondence and Papers, 1796–1802*, ed. David Preston (Bloomsbury, 2011), 301–4 (emphasis added).
42. Quoted in Rosemarie Zagarri, *A Woman's Dilemma: Mercy Otis Warren and the American Revolution* (John Wiley & Sons, 2015), 126.
43. Thomas Jefferson to James Madison, 9 June 1793, FOL.
44. David S. Heidler and Jeanne T. Heidler, *Washington's Circle: The Creation of the President* (Random House, 2015), 285.
45. GW to Boston Selectmen, 28 July 1795, FOL.
46. GW to the Citizens of Baltimore, 17 April 1789, *PGWP* 2:62–65.
47. I wish to acknowledge Joseph Ellis for this insight.
48. This is carefully examined in Spalding and Garrity, *A Sacred Union of Citizens*.

49. Heidler and Heidler, *Washington's Circle*, 392.
50. Stewart, *George Washington*, 11.
51. I wish to credit Gordon Wood for this insight.
52. Cogliano, *A Revolutionary Friendship*, 248.

7. The Final Years

1. John Adams to Abigail Adams, 5 March 1797, FOL.
2. GW to James Anderson (of Scotland), 7 April 1797, FOL.
3. GW to the Earl of Buchan, 4 July 1797, FOL.
4. John Adams to Benjamin Rush, 12 June 1812, FOL.
5. W. W. Abbot, "George Washington in Retirement," Lowell Lecture Series, 5 December 1999, https://washingtonpapers.org/resources/articles/george-washington-in-retirement/.
6. GW to James McHenry, 3 April 1797, FOL.
7. Thomas Jefferson to Philip Mazzei, 24 April 1796, FOL.
8. All of the marginalia are found in the editorial note in *The Papers of George Washington*, "Comments on Monroe's A View of the Conduct of the Executive of the United States," March 1798, FOL.
9. GW to Charles Carroll (of Carrollton), 2 August 1798, FOL.
10. GW to Marquis de Lafayette, 25 December 1798, *PGWRT* 3:108–10. See also Ellis, *His Excellency*, 246.
11. GW to Alexander Hamilton, 29 July 1795, FOL.
12. Abbot, "George Washington in Retirement."
13. GW to James Lloyd, 15 April 1798, *PGWRT* 2:241.
14. Editorial notes *PGWRT* 2:127.
15. John Adams to GW, 22 June 1798, FOL.
16. GW to John Adams, 17 June 1798, *PGWRT* 2:334.
17. GW to James McHenry, 4 July 1798, FOL.
18. GW to James McHenry, 4 July 1798, FOL.
19. GW to Alexander Hamilton, 27 May 1798, *PGWRT* 2:297.
20. GW to James McHenry, 4 July 1798, FOL.
21. GW to Alexander Hamilton, 27 May 1798, *PGWRT* 2:297.
22. GW to John Adams, 25 September 1798, FOL.
23. Lindsay M. Chervinsky, *Making the Presidency: John Adams and the Precedents That Forged the Republic* (Oxford University Press, 2024), 157. She asserted, "It was one of the worst choices made by Washington in his long and storied public career."
24. John Adams to James Lloyd, 12 February 1815, FOL.
25. John Adams to James McHenry, 29 August 1798, FOL.
26. John Adams to Benjamin Rush, 11 November 1807, FOL.
27. GW to William Fitzhugh, 5 August 1798, FOL.
28. GW to James McAlpin, 27 January 1799, *PGWRT* 3:340–42, quote on 341.
29. This is well covered in Chervinsky, *Making the Presidency*.

30. GW to Jonathan Trumbull Jr., 21 July 1799, FOL.
31. John Adams to Benjamin Rush, 12 June 1812, FOL.
32. GW to Lawrence Lewis, 28 September 1799, *PGWRT* 4:325.
33. Quoted in Cunliffe, *Man and Monument*, 132.
34. Thomas Jefferson to Walter Jones, 2 January 1814, FOL.
35. Reverend John McVickar, *A Domestic Narrative of the Life of Samuel Bard*, quoted in George Washington Nordham, *George Washington's Religious Faith* (Adams, 1986), 28–29.
36. GW to Burwell Bassett, 20 June 1773, *PGWCL* 9:243.
37. All of these references are cited in Peter R. Henriques, "The Final Struggle between George Washington and the Grim King: Washington's Attitude toward Death and an Afterlife," *Virginia Magazine of History and Biography* 107 (1999): 73–97.
38. GW to Henry Knox, 27 April 1787, *PGWCF* 5:157 (emphasis added).
39. GW to Betty Washington Lewis, 13 September 1789, *PGWP* 4:32 (emphasis added).
40. GW to Marquis de Lafayette, 8 December 1784, *PGWCF* 2:175 (emphasis added).
41. GW to James Anderson, 13 December 1799, *PGWRT* 4:455–77.
42. Tobias Lear to Mary Stillson Lear, 16 December 1799. Copy in information file on GW's death. Mount Vernon Ladies' Association.
43. Tobias Lear, Diary Account, *PGWRT* 4:547.
44. This point is made by Joel Achenbach, *The Grand Idea: George Washington's Potomac and the Race to the West* (Simon & Schuster, 2005).
45. The quote is from the 1968 play *The Lion in Winter,* by James Goldman.
46. GW to Burgess Ball, 22 September 1799, *PGWRT* 4:318.
47. I examine GW's death in more detail in *Realistic Visionary,* chap. 10.
48. Tobias Lear; Journal Account, *PGWRT* 4:543.
49. The quote is taken from Smith, *Patriarch,* 353.
50. George Washington's Last Will and Testament, *PGWRT* 4:477–92.
51. William Gordon to GW, 30 August 1784, *PGWCF* 2:64.
52. Ellis, *His Excellency,* 269.
53. Lear, Journal Account, *PGWRT* 4:545.
54. Bryan Fairfax to the Earl of Buchan, 28 January 1800, copy in information file, MVLA.
55. Lear, Diary Account, *PGWRT* 4:545.
56. Lear, Diary Account, *PGWRT* 4:545.
57. William Martin, *Citizen Washington: A Novel* (Grand Central, 1999), 574.
58. Thomas Jefferson to Walter Jones, 2 January 1814, FOL.

Afterword

1. Zagarri, *Life of Washington by Humphreys,* 78.
2. GW to Alexander Spotswood, 23 November 1794, FOL.

3. Philip Roth, *The Human Stain* (Houghton Mifflin, 2000), 2.
4. Maurizio Valsania, *First Among Men: George Washington and the Myth of American Masculinity* (Johns Hopkins University Press, 2022), 80. The author meant that Washington is "not one of us" in several different ways, but clearly a major way was his attitude toward race and slavery. I believe the clearest example of the author being unable to understand Washington's worldview regarding slavery comes from his comment about Washington showing a worker that though he has his arm in a sling, he can still work. "How could this intelligent man not grasp that, morally, it didn't make any difference whether in this case the injury was real or just pretended? Deception was not the issue, as the poor man had the moral right to resist the cruel joke and make his burden a little easier" (77). Washington would never have considered this point of view.
5. GW to Joseph Thompson, 2 July 1776, PGWCL 7:453–54.
6. GW to Hector Ross, 9 October 1769, FOL.
7. Thompson, *The Only Unavoidable Subject of Regret*, 64.
8. This sentence is a composite from material in chapter 8, "Regrets at Mount Vernon," and Joseph Ellis's forthcoming book *Realities and Regrets: The Tragic Side of the Founding*. I am very grateful to him for allowing me access to this material.
9. William Ferraro, an editor of *The Papers of George Washington*, sent me sections of volume 34 of the Revolutionary Series, which was not yet published. I am deeply in his debt for his help.
10. GW to François-Joseph-Paul, Comte de Grasse-Tilly, 6 February 1782, FOL.
11. GW to William Fitzhugh, 8 February 1782, FOL.
12. Chernow, *Washington*, 42.
13. GW to James McHenry, 11 November 1786, *PGWCF* 4:358–59.
14. GW to Joseph Whipple, 28 November 1796, FOL.
15. GW to Oliver Wolcott Jr., 1 September 1796, FOL.
16. Henry Wiencek, *An Imperfect God: George Washington, His Slaves, and the Creation of America* (Farrar, Straus and Giroux, 2003), 324.
17. The most complete treatment of this fascinating story is Erica Armstrong Dunbar, *Never Caught: The Washingtons' Relentless Pursuit of Their Runaway Slave, Ona Judge* (Atria Books, 2017). On occasion, the book reads more like historical fiction. For example, a careful reading of the available evidence indicates that Burwell Bassett likely never had a direct confrontation with Ona, which was so vividly portrayed in the book (165–66).
18. GW to Tobias Lear, 12 April 1791, FOL.
19. GW to James Anderson, 20 February 1797, FOL.
20. GW to John Fairfax, 1 January 1789, FOL. The two following quotes come from the same letter.
21. GW to Anthony Whitting, 16 December 1792, FOL.
22. GW to James Anderson, 20 February 1797, FOL.
23. GW to Bryan Fairfax, 24 August 1774, FOL.

24. James C. Nicholls, "Lady Henrietta Liston's Journal of Washington's 'Resignation,' Retirement, and Death," *Pennsylvania Magazine of History and Biography* 95, no. 4 (1971): 515.
25. Quoted in Valsania, *First Among Men,* 76.
26. GW to Anthony Whitting, 16 December 1792, FOL.
27. Anthony Whitting to GW, 16 January 1793, FOL.
28. GW to Anthony Whitting, 20 January 1793, FOL.
29. Thompson, *The Only Unavoidable Subject of Regret,* 252.
30. Thompson, *The Only Unavoidable Subject of Regret,* 252.
31. GW to Robert Morris, 12 April 1786, FOL. It is worth noting that Washington made this statement in a letter devoted to a strong condemnation of Quaker efforts to assist slaves in claiming their rights under Pennsylvania law. I wish to acknowledge Bruce Ragsdale for this information.
32. Quoted in John Bernard, *Retrospections of America, 1797–1811* (Harper & Brothers, 1887), 88, 90–91.
33. GW to Alexander Spotswood, 23 November 1794, FOL.
34. François Furstenberg, "Some Reflections on George Washington and Slavery," lecture delivered to the Maryland Senate, February 17, 2020, https://msa.maryland.gov/msa/mdstatehouse/pdf/2020-02-17remarks.pdf.
35. Bruce A. Ragsdale, *Washington at the Plow: The Founding Father and the Question of Slavery* (Harvard University Press, 2021).
36. I wish to credit David Stewart with this observation.
37. Ellis, *His Excellency,* 258.
38. GW to David Stuart, 15 June 1790, FOL.
39. GW to Robert Morris, 12 April 1786, FOL.
40. George Washington's Last Will and Testament, 9 July 1799, FOL.
41. Furstenberg, *In the Name of the Father,* 84.
42. Ellis, *His Excellency,* 264.
43. Ellis, *His Excellency,* 151–52.
44. Zagarri, *Life of Washington by Humphreys,* 78. This is a very famous quote, but it is likely not exactly what Washington said. Humphreys, strongly antislavery himself, admitted that he had a very strong interest in Washington's reputation and may have massaged Washington's words for maximum effect (see David Humphreys to GW, 17 July 1785).
45. George Washington's Last Will and Testament, 9 July 1799, FOL (emphasis added).
46. Furstenberg, *In the Name of the Father,* 88.
47. I wish to credit Bruce Ragsdale for this insight.
48. Ellis, *His Excellency,* 158.
49. GW to Phillis Wheatley, 22 February 1776, FOL.
50. I wish to credit Bruce Ragsdale for this insight.
51. Wills, *Cincinnatus,* 235.

INDEX

"GW" refers to George Washington and "MW" to Martha Washington. Page numbers in italics refer to illustrations.